EASY PIANO SELECTIONS

# CATS

MUSIC FROM THE MOTION
PICTURE SOUNDTRACK

T0055756

2  JELLICLE SONGS FOR JELLICLE CATS

16  THE OLD GUMBIE CAT

9  THE RUM TUM TUGGER

22  BUSTOPHER JONES: THE CAT ABOUT TOWN

35  MUNGOJERRIE AND RUMPLETEAZER

44  OLD DEUTERONOMY

30  BEAUTIFUL GHOSTS

48  GUS: THE THEATRE CAT

64  SKIMBLESHANKS: THE RAILWAY CAT

55  MACAVITY: THE MYSTERY CAT

73  MR. MISTOFFELEES

78  MEMORY

82  THE AD-DRESSING OF CATS

ISBN 978-1-5400-8674-7

For all works contained herein:
Unauthorized copying, arranging, adapting, recording, Internet posting, public performance,
or other distribution of the music in this publication is an infringement of copyright.
Infringers are liable under the law.

The musical works contained in this edition may not be publicly performed
in a dramatic form or context except under license from
The Really Useful Group Limited, 17 Slingsby Place, London WC2E 9AB

Visit Hal Leonard Online at
**www.halleonard.com**

Contact us:
**Hal Leonard**
7777 West Bluemound Road
Milwaukee, WI 53213
Email: info@halleonard.com

In Europe, contact:
**Hal Leonard Europe Limited**
42 Wigmore Street
Marylebone, London, W1U 2RN
Email: info@halleonardeurope.com

In Australia, contact:
**Hal Leonard Australia Pty. Ltd.**
4 Lentara Court
Cheltenham, Victoria, 3192 Australia
Email: info@halleonard.com.au

# JELLICLE SONGS FOR JELLICLE CATS

Music by ANDREW LLOYD WEBBER
Text by TREVOR NUNN
and RICHARD STILGOE after T.S. ELIOT

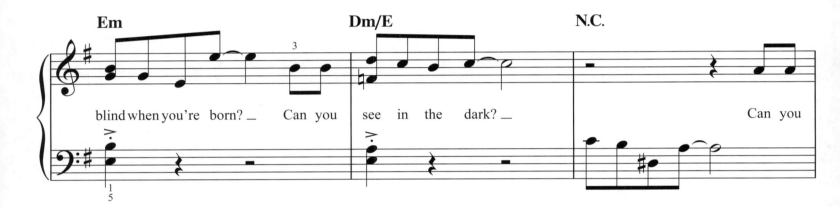

Music Copyright © 1981 Andrew Lloyd Webber licensed to The Really Useful Group Ltd.
Text Copyright © 1981 Trevor Nunn, Richard Stilgoe and Set Copyrights Ltd.
All Rights in the text Controlled by Faber and Faber Ltd.
International Copyright Secured   All Rights Reserved

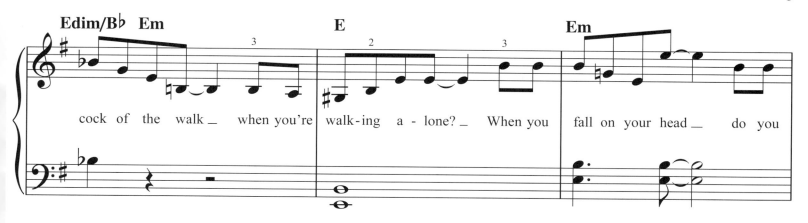

cock of the walk _ when you're walk-ing a - lone? _ When you fall on your head _ do you

land on your feet? _ Are you tense when you sense _ there's a

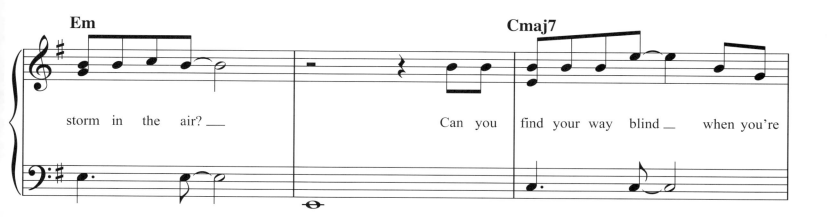

storm in the air? _ Can you find your way blind _ when you're

lost in the street? Do you know how to go _ to the heav-y-side layer? Be-cause

*mf*

4

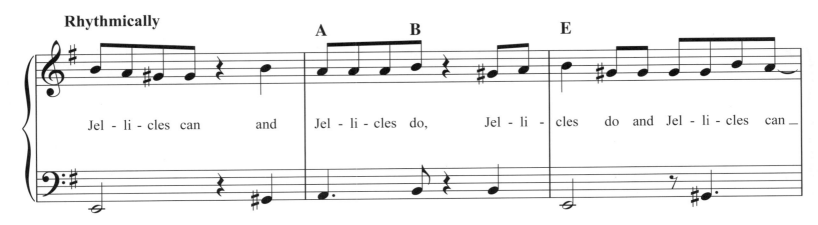

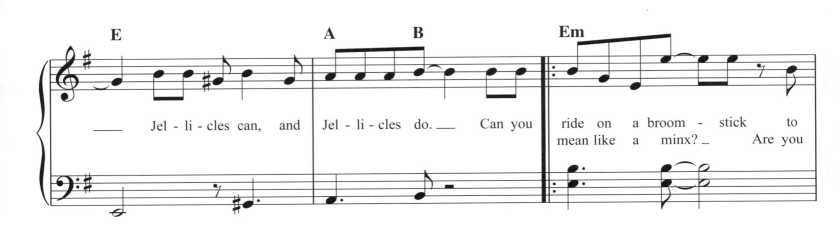

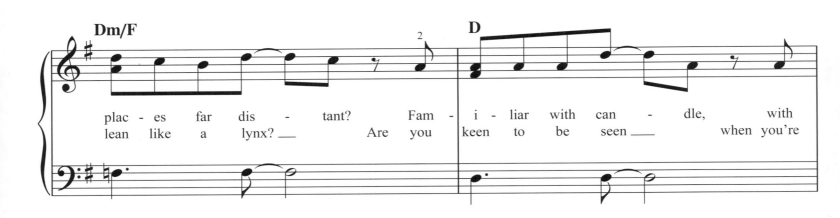

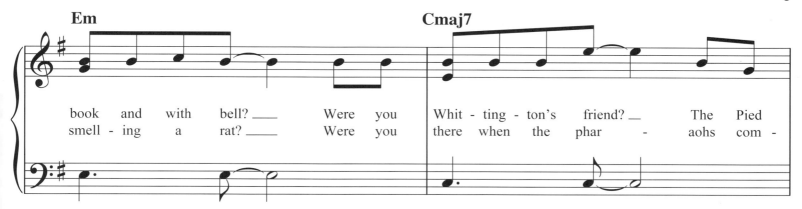

book and with bell? ___ Were you Whit - ting - ton's friend? __ The Pied
smell - ing a rat? ___ Were you there when the phar - aohs com -

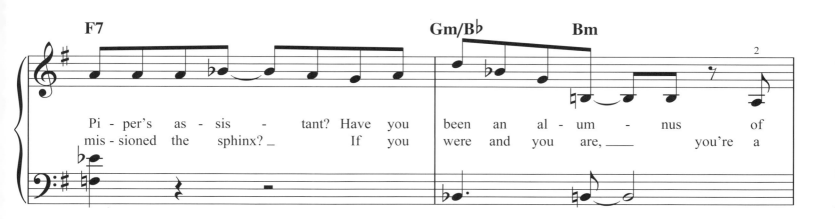

Pi - per's as - sis - tant? Have you been an al - um - nus of
mis - sioned the sphinx? _ If you were and you are, ___ you're a

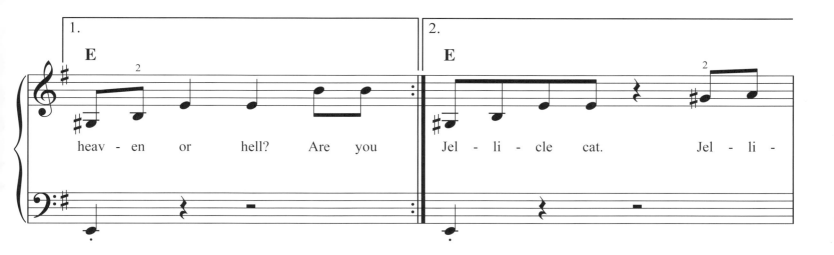

1.
heav - en or hell? Are you

2.
Jel - li - cle cat. Jel - li -

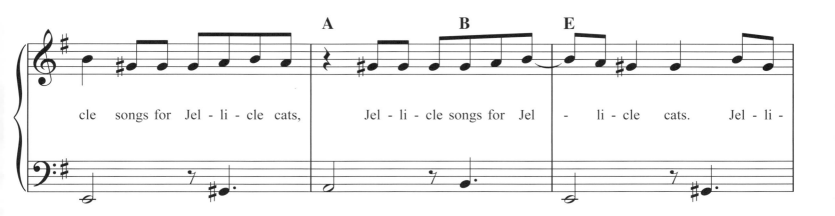

cle songs for Jel - li - cle cats, Jel - li - cle songs for Jel - li - cle cats. Jel - li -

6

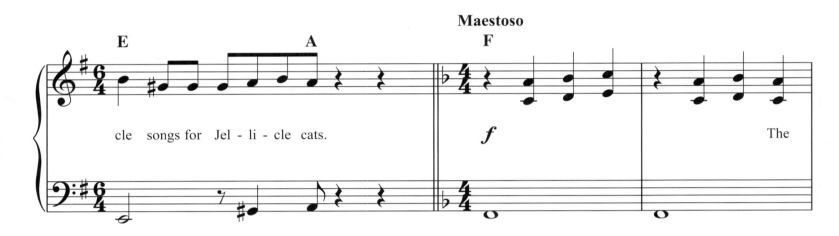

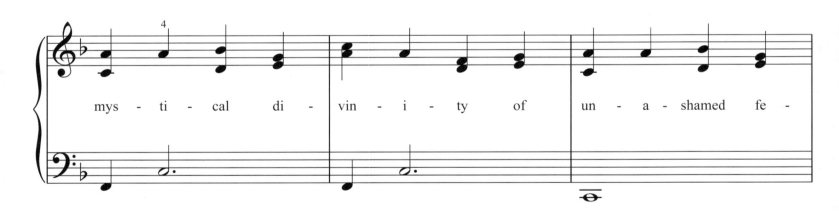

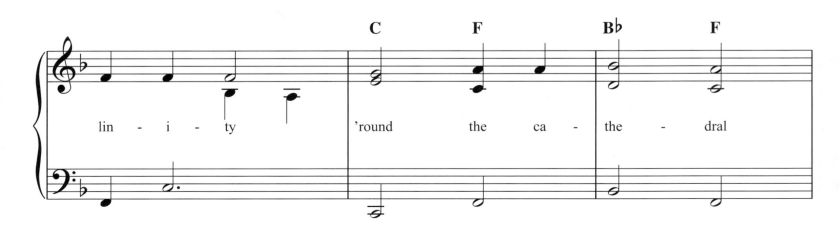

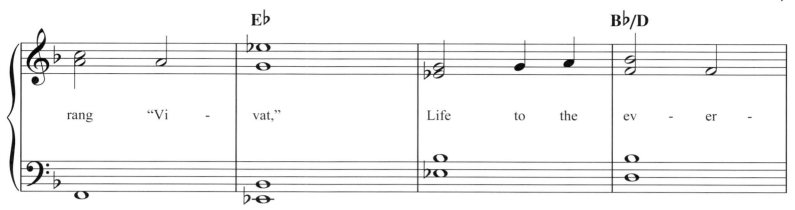

rang "Vi - vat," Life to the ev - er -

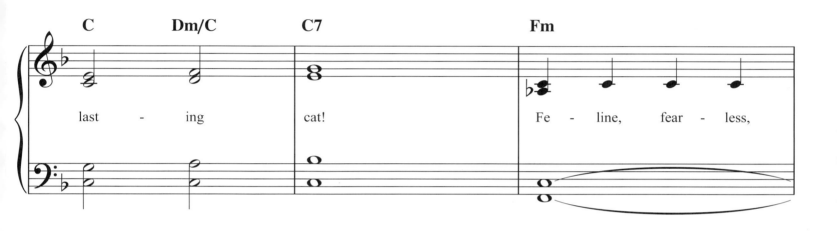

last - ing cat! Fe - line, fear - less,

**Rhythmically, as before**

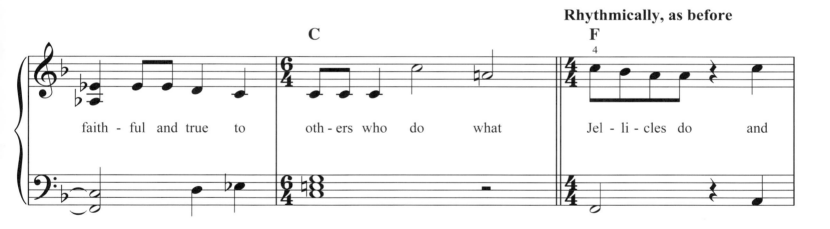

faith - ful and true to oth - ers who do what Jel - li - cles do and

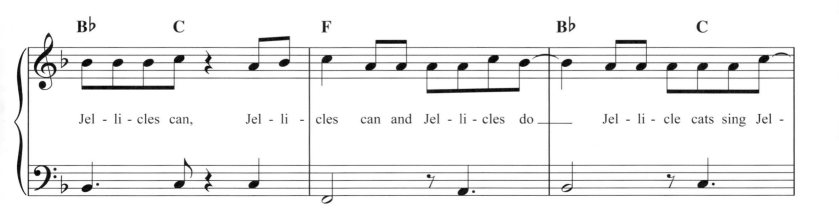

Jel - li - cles can, Jel - li - cles can and Jel - li - cles do___ Jel - li - cle cats sing Jel -

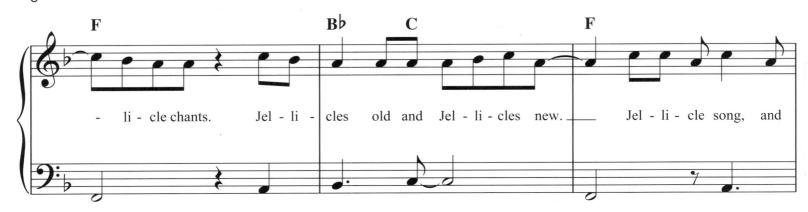

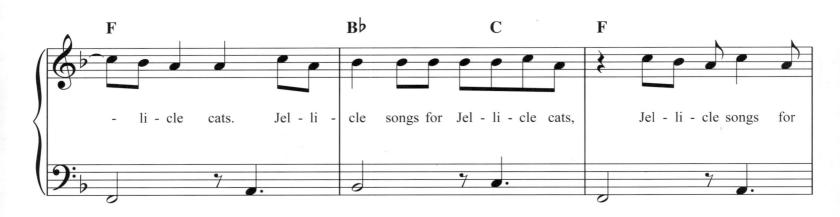

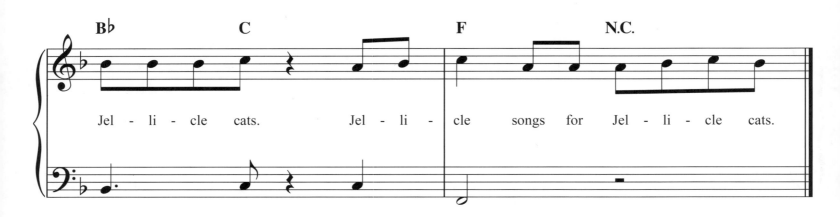

# THE RUM TUM TUGGER

Music by ANDREW LLOYD WEBBER
Text by T.S. ELIOT

**Moderately fast**

Rum Tum Tug - ger is a cur - i - ous cat. If you
Rum Tum Tug - ger is a ter - ri - ble bore.

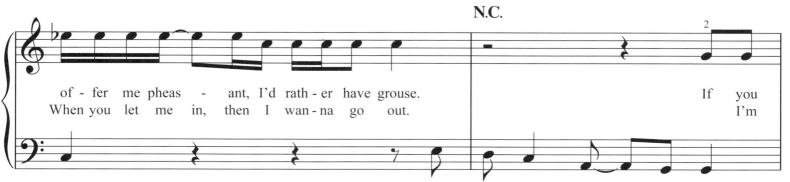

of - fer me pheas - ant, I'd rath - er have grouse. If you
When you let me in, then I wan-na go out. I'm

Music Copyright © 1980 Andrew Lloyd Webber licensed to The Really Useful Group Ltd.
Text Copyright © 1939 T.S. Eliot; this edition of the text © 1980 Set Copyrights Ltd.
All Rights in the text Controlled by Faber and Faber Ltd.
International Copyright Secured   All Rights Reserved

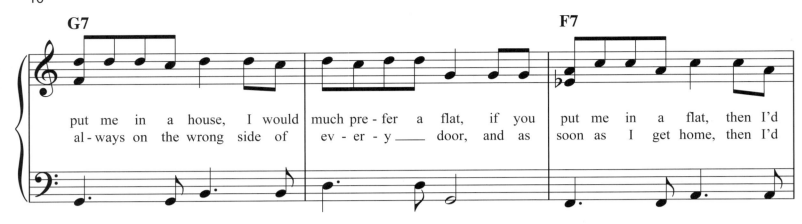

put me in a house, I would | much pre - fer a flat, if you | put me in a flat, then I'd
al - ways on the wrong side of | ev - er - y ____ door, and as | soon as I get home, then I'd

rath - er have a house. ____ If you | set me on a mouse, then I
like to get a - bout. ____ I ____ | like ____ to ____ lie in the

on - ly want a rat. ____ If you | set me on a rat, then I'd rath - er chase a mouse.
bur - eau ____ drawer. ____ But I | make ___ such a fuss if I can't ___ get ___ out.

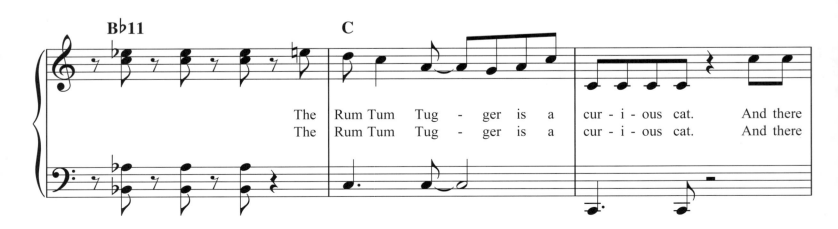

The Rum Tum Tug - ger is a | cur - i - ous cat. And there
The Rum Tum Tug - ger is a | cur - i - ous cat. And there

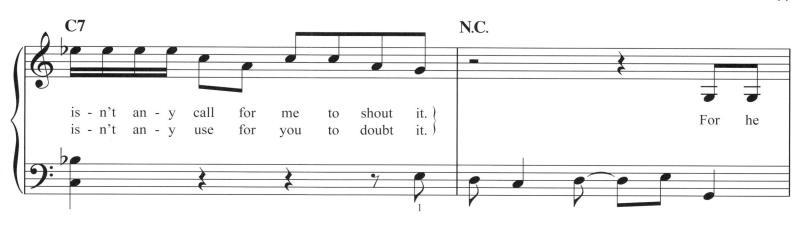

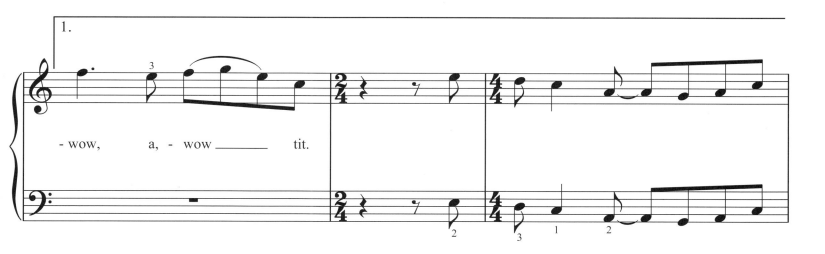

**2.**

wow,   a, - wow _____ tit.   The

**C7#9**

**C**

Rum Tum Tug - ger is a   cur - i - ous beast.   My

**C7#9**

dis - o - blig - ing ways are a mat - ter of hab - it.   If you

**N.C.**

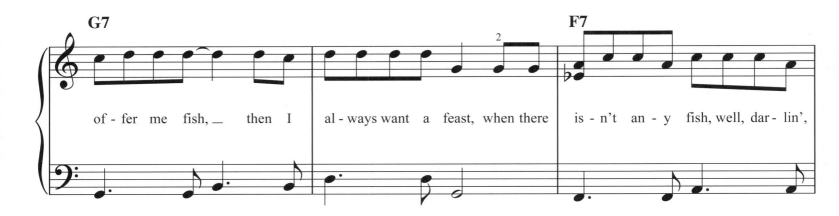

**G7**

of - fer me fish, __ then I   al - ways want a feast, when there   is - n't an - y fish, well, dar - lin',

**F7**

nothing I en-joy like a hor-ri-ble mud-dle.

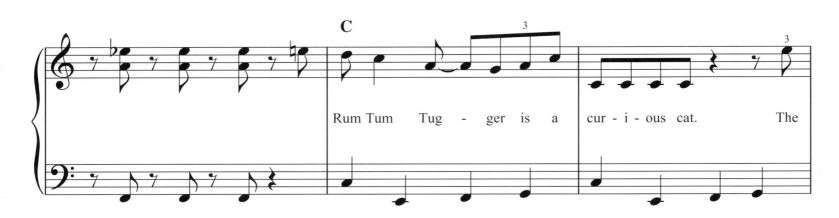

Rum Tum Tug - ger is a cur - i - ous cat. The

Rum Tum Tug - ger does-n't care for a cud - dle.

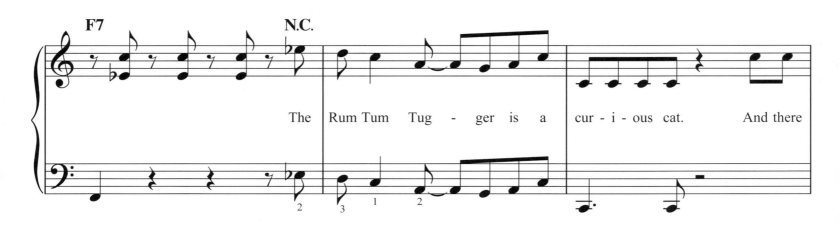

The Rum Tum Tug - ger is a cur - i - ous cat. And there

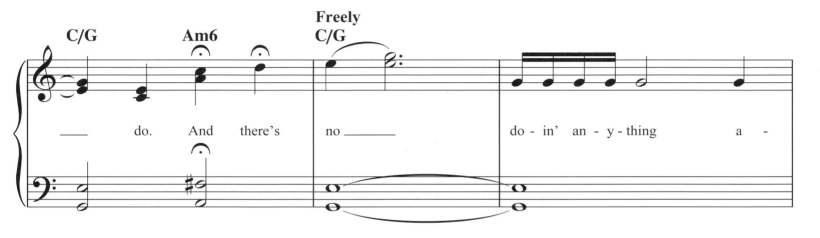

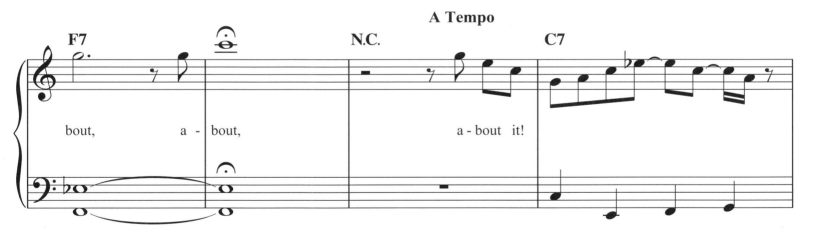

# THE OLD GUMBIE CAT

Music by ANDREW LLOYD WEBBER
Text by T.S. ELIOT

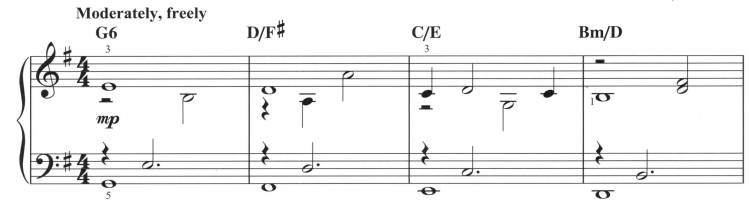

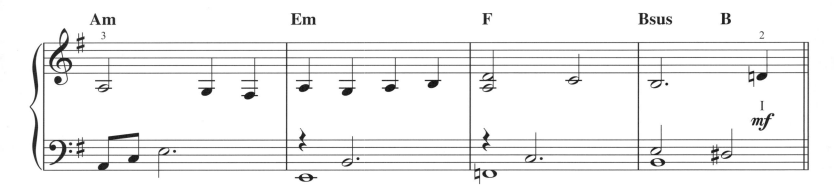

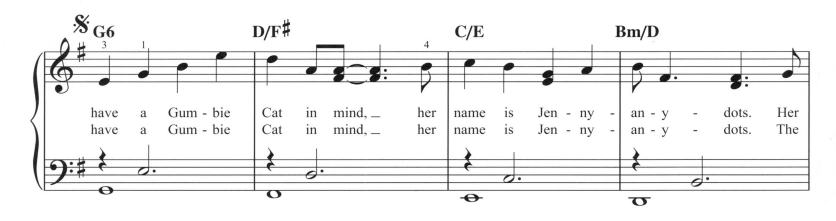

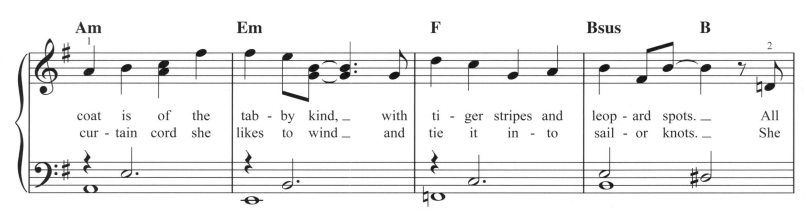

Music Copyright © 1981 Andrew Lloyd Webber licensed to The Really Useful Group Ltd.
Text Copyright © 1939 T.S. Eliot; this edition of the text © 1981 Set Copyrights Ltd.
All Rights in the text Controlled by Faber and Faber Ltd.
International Copyright Secured   All Rights Reserved

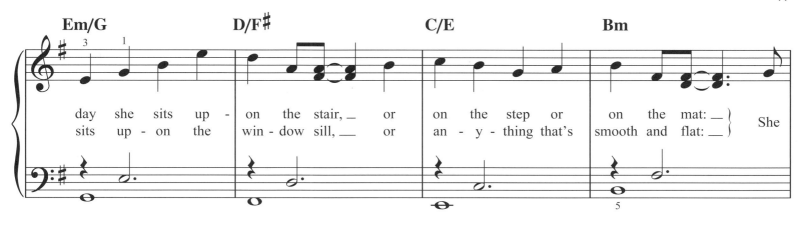

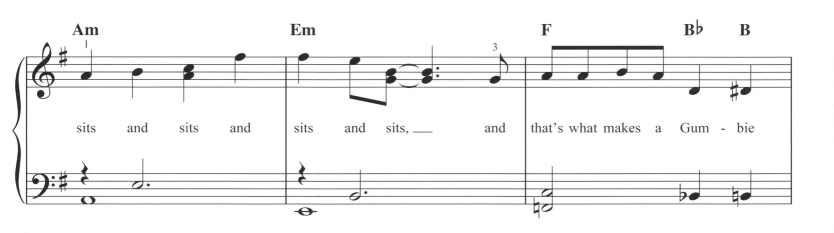

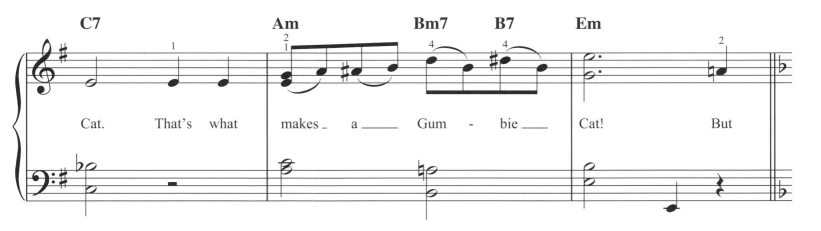

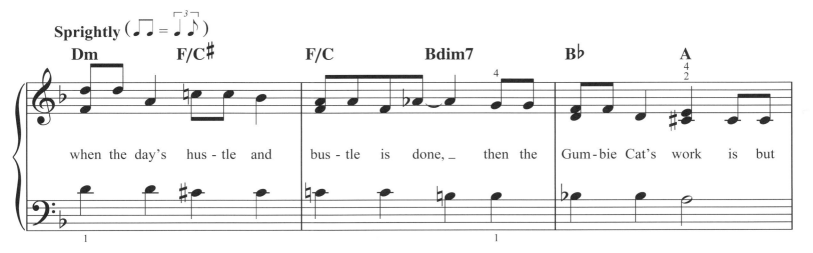

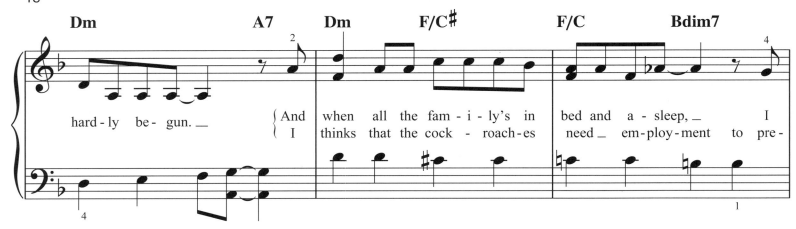

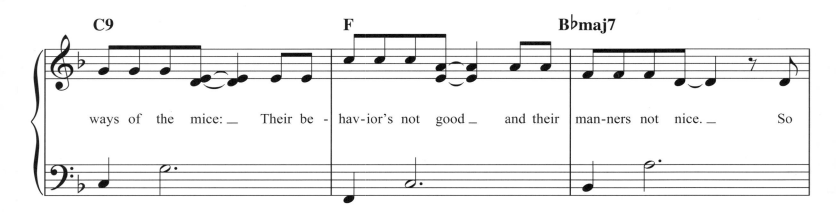

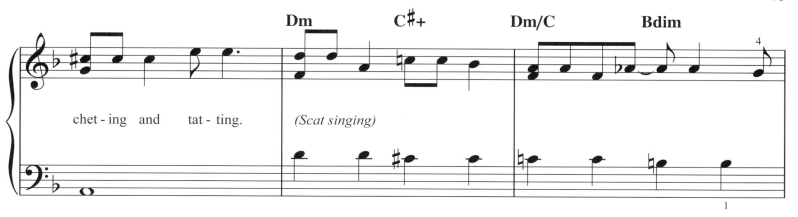

chet - ing and tat - ting. *(Scat singing)*

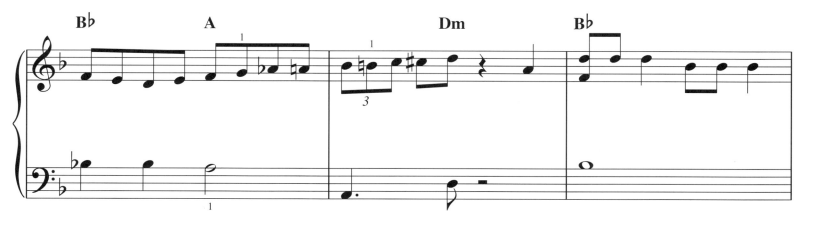

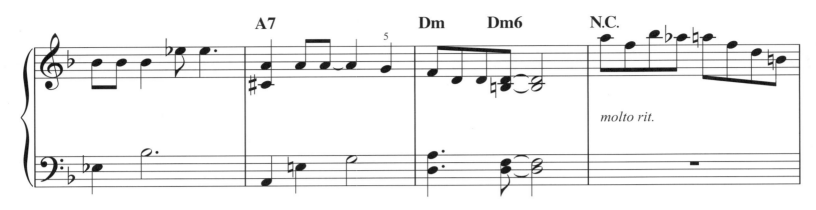

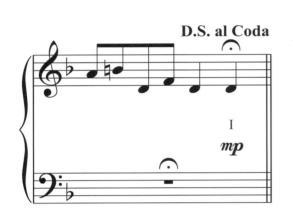
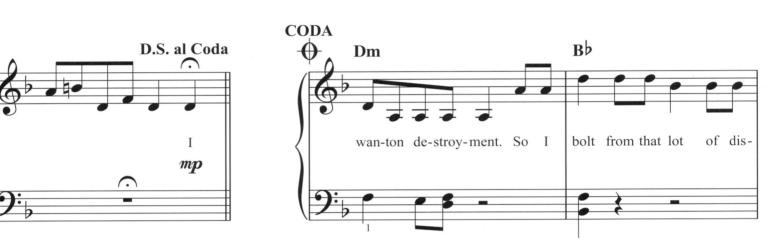

wan-ton de-stroy-ment. So I bolt from that lot of dis-

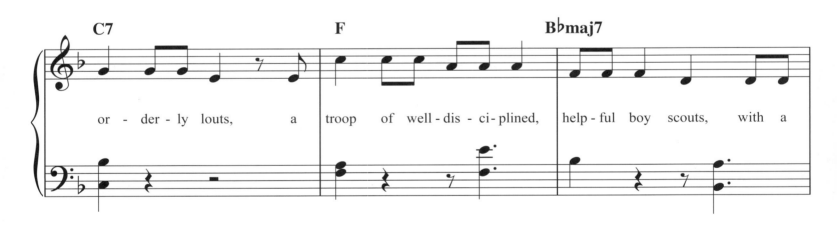

or-der-ly louts,  a  troop  of well-dis-ci-plined,  help-ful boy scouts,  with a

pur-pose in  life  and  a  good deed  to  do;  and I've  e-ven  cre-

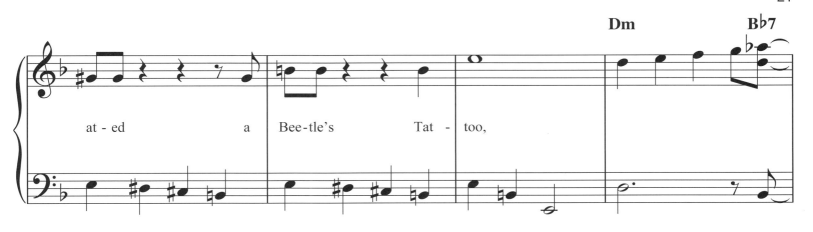

at-ed a Bee-tle's Tat-too,

So for Old Gum-bie Cats, let us now give three cheers, _ on whom

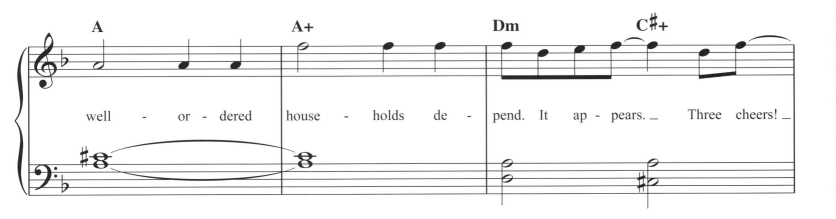

well - or-dered house-holds de-pend. It ap-pears. _ Three cheers! _

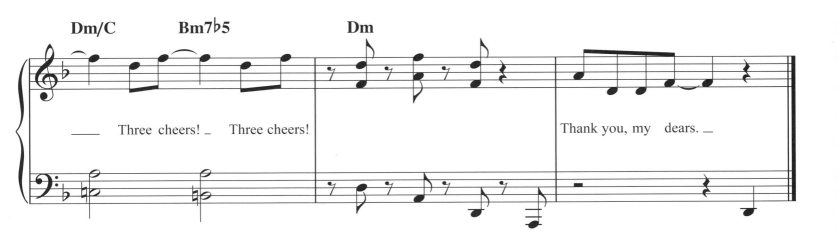

_ Three cheers! _ Three cheers! Thank you, my dears. _

# BUSTOPHER JONES: THE CAT ABOUT TOWN

Music by ANDREW LLOYD WEBBER
Text by T.S. ELIOT

I'm Bus-to-pher Jones. I'm not skin and bones. In fact, I'm re-mark-a-bly fat. I don't haunt pubs, I have eight or nine clubs for I'm the Saint James-'s Street cat! I'm the

Music Copyright © 1980 Andrew Lloyd Webber licensed to The Really Useful Group Ltd.
Text Copyright © 1939 T.S. Eliot; this edition of the text © 1980 Set Copyrights Ltd.
All Rights in the text Controlled by Faber and Faber Ltd.
International Copyright Secured All Rights Reserved

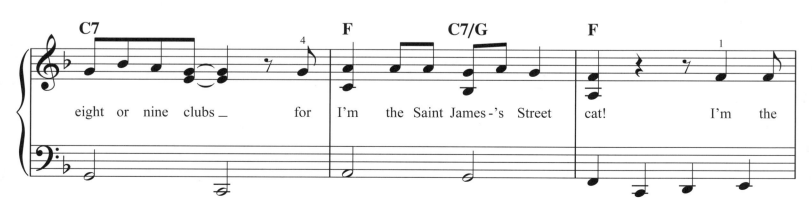

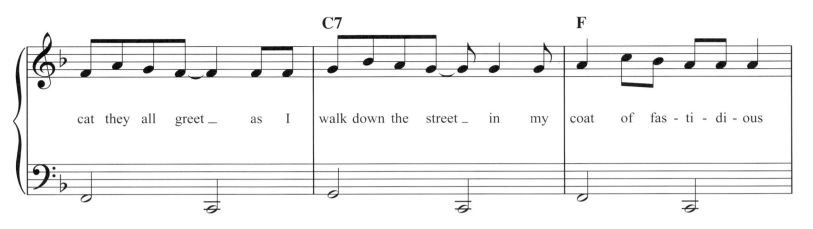

cat they all greet _ as I | walk down the street _ in my | coat of fas - ti - di - ous

black. | No com-mon-place mous _ ers have | such well - cut trous _ ers or

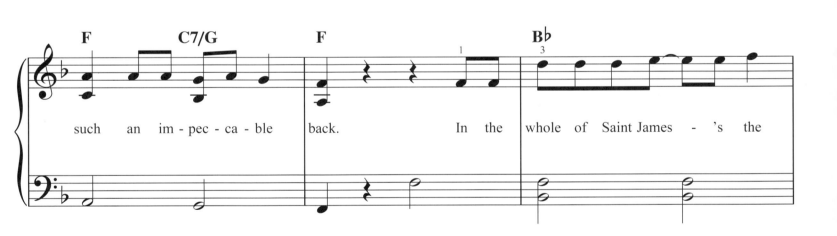

such an im - pec - ca - ble | back. In the | whole of Saint James _ 's the

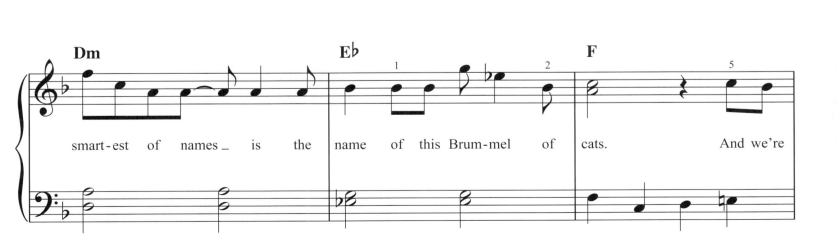

smart-est of names _ is the | name of this Brum-mel of | cats. And we're

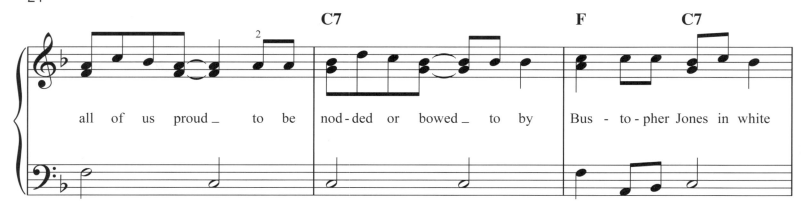

all of us proud _ to be nod-ded or bowed _ to by Bus - to-pher Jones in white

**Slightly slower (♩♩ = ♩♩)**

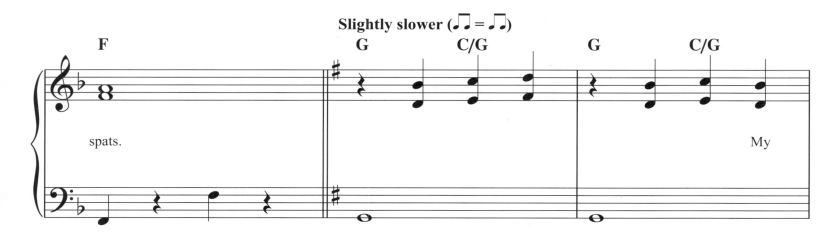

spats. My

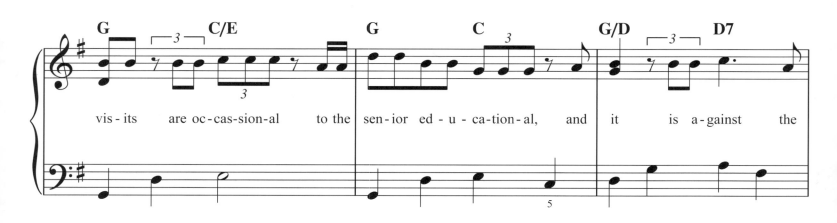

vis - its are oc-cas-sion-al to the sen-ior ed - u - ca-tion-al, and it is a-gainst the

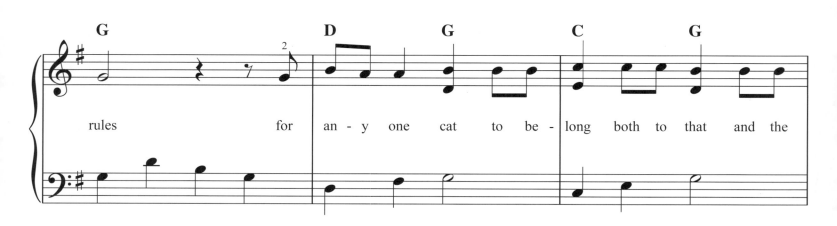

rules for an - y one cat to be - long both to that and the

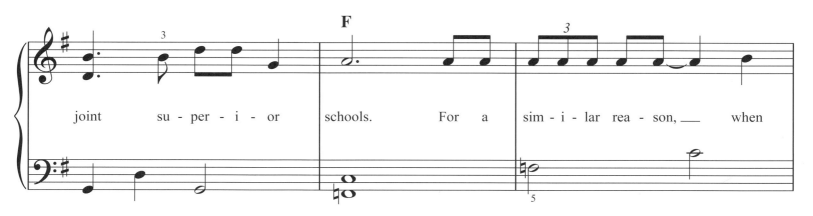

joint su – per – i – or schools. For a sim – i – lar rea – son, ___ when

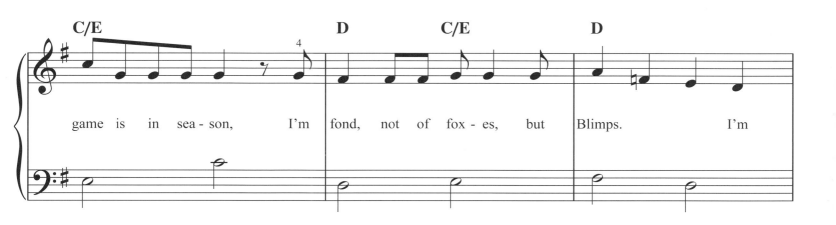

game is in sea – son, I'm fond, not of fox – es, but Blimps. I'm

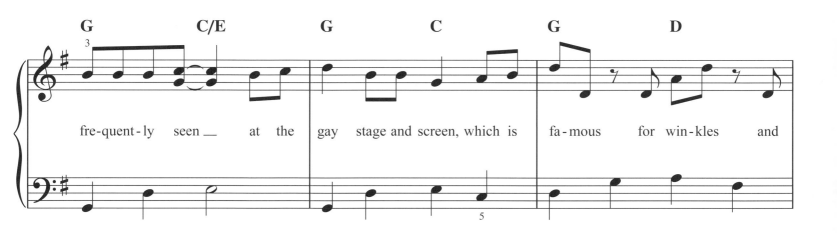

fre – quent – ly seen ___ at the gay stage and screen, which is fa – mous for win – kles and

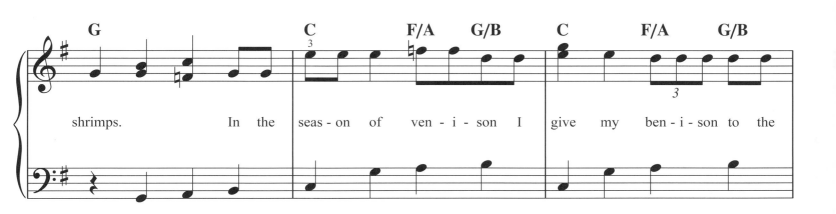

shrimps. In the seas – on of ven – i – son I give my ben – i – son to the

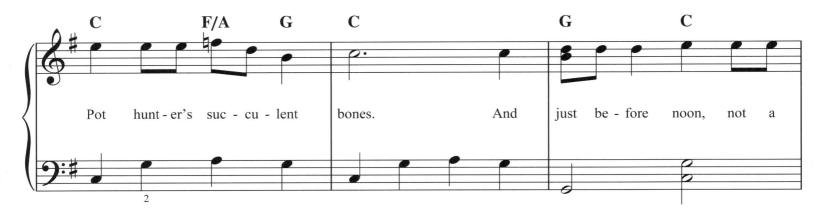

Pot hunt - er's suc - cu - lent bones. And just be - fore noon, not a

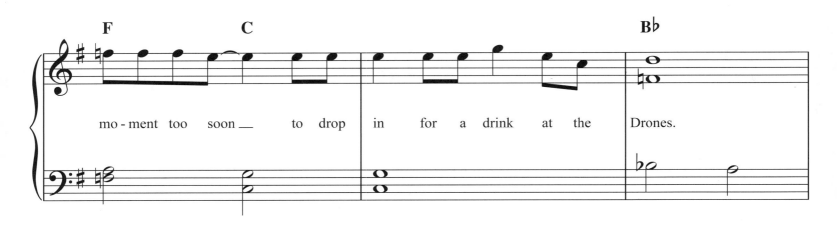

mo - ment too soon ___ to drop in for a drink at the Drones.

When I'm seen in a hur - ry, there's prob - a - bly cur - ry at the

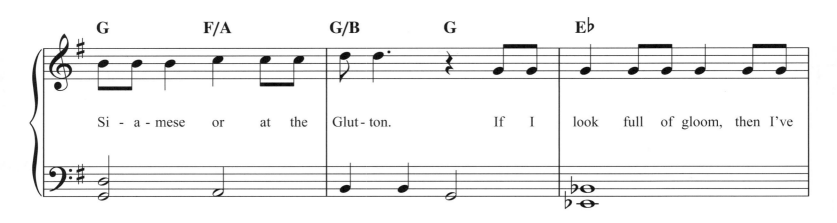

Si - a - mese or at the Glut - ton. If I look full of gloom, then I've

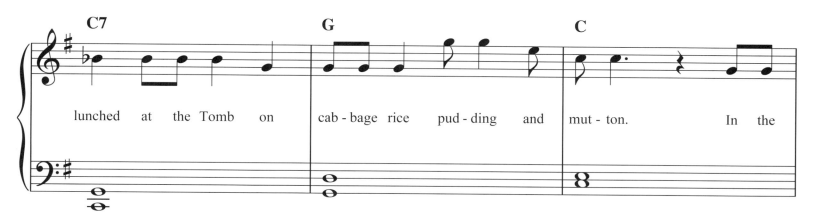

lunched at the Tomb on cab-bage rice pud-ding and mut-ton. In the

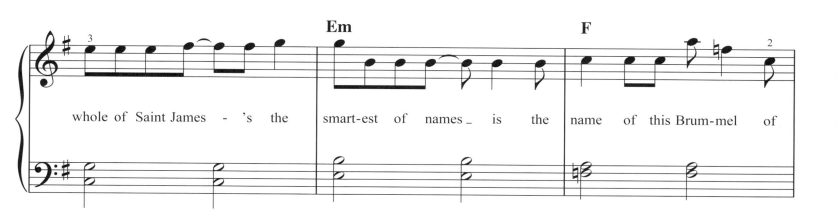

whole of Saint James - 's the smart-est of names _ is the name of this Brum-mel of

cats. And we're all of us proud _ to be nod-ded or bowed _ to by

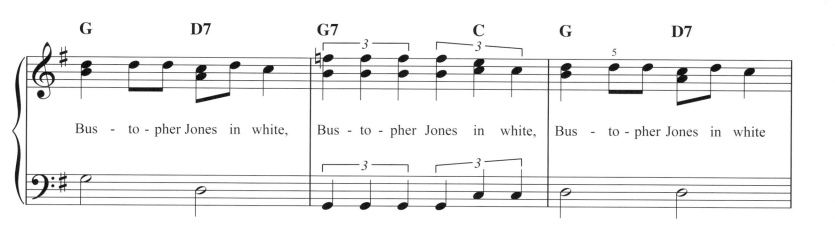

Bus - to - pher Jones in white, Bus - to - pher Jones in white, Bus - to - pher Jones in white

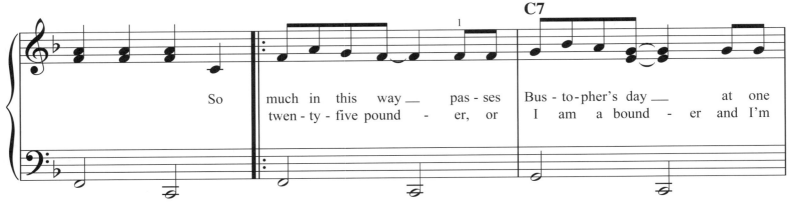

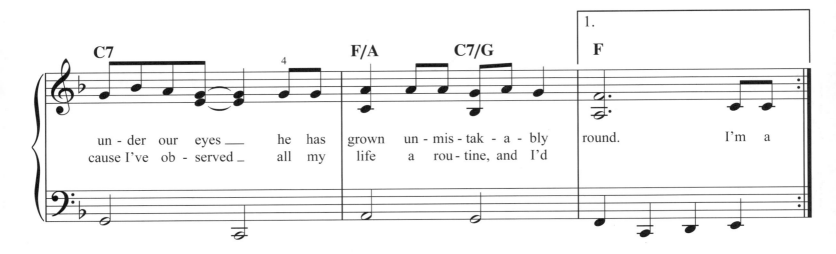

say, I am still in my prime; I shall last out my time. That's the

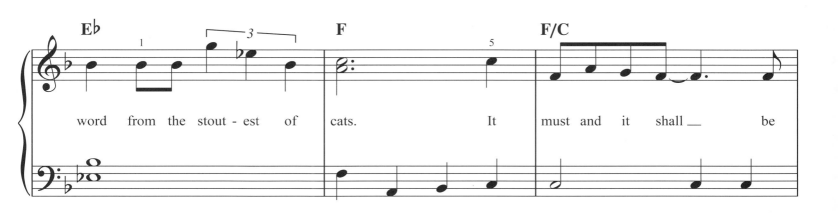

word from the stout-est of cats. It must and it shall ___ be

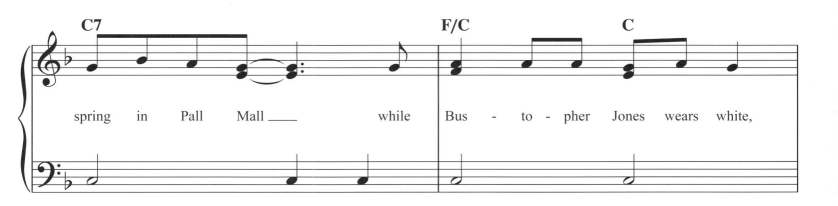

spring in Pall Mall ____ while Bus - to - pher Jones wears white,

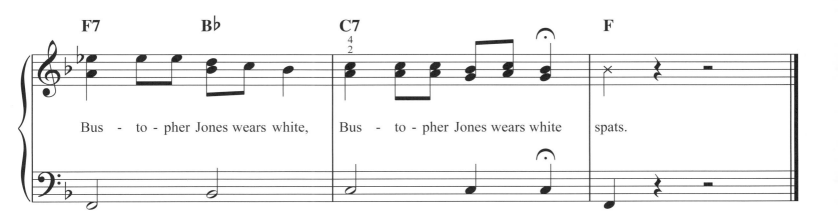

Bus - to - pher Jones wears white, Bus - to - pher Jones wears white spats.

# BEAUTIFUL GHOSTS

Words and Music by TAYLOR SWIFT
and ANDREW LLOYD WEBBER

Copyright © 2019 Sony/ATV Music Publishing LLC, Taylor Swift Music and The Really Useful Group Ltd.
All Rights on behalf of Sony/ATV Music Publishing LLC and Taylor Swift Music Administered by Sony/ATV Music Publishing LLC, 424 Church Street, Suite 1200, Nashville, TN 37219
International Copyright Secured   All Rights Reserved

watch from the dark, wait for my life to start, with no beau - ty in my mem - o -
call them my friends and be bro - ken a - gain. Is this hope just a mys - ti - cal

ry.
dream? }

(1., 2.) All that I want - ed
(D.S.) All that I want - ed

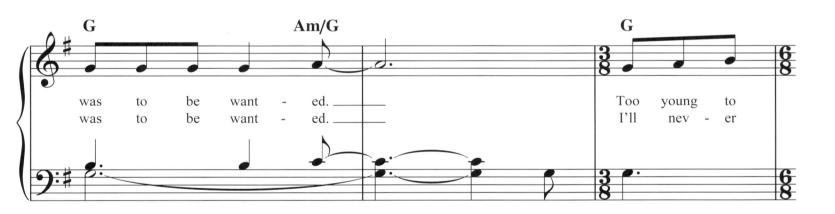

was to be want - ed. Too young to
was to be want - ed. I'll nev - er

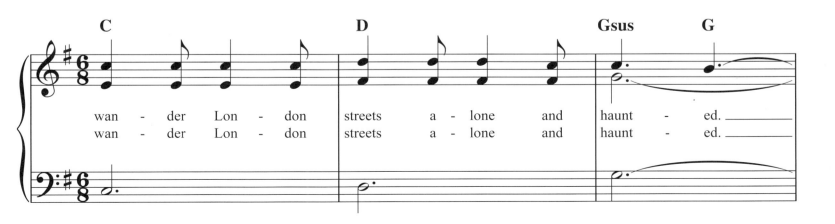

wan - der Lon - don streets a - lone and haunt - ed.
wan - der Lon - don streets a - lone and haunt - ed.

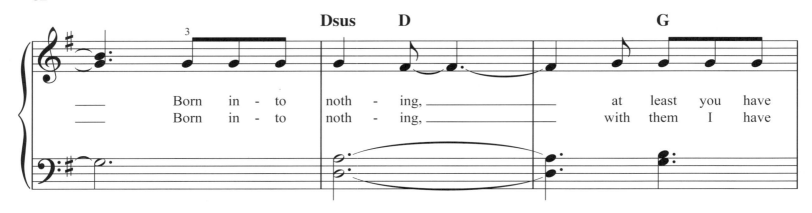

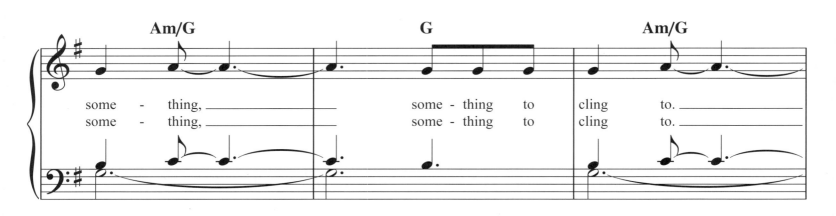

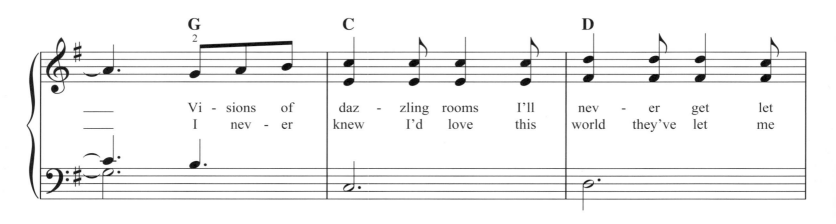

phan-toms of night. And I know that this life is-n't safe, but it's wild and it's

free. ghosts. ____ And the

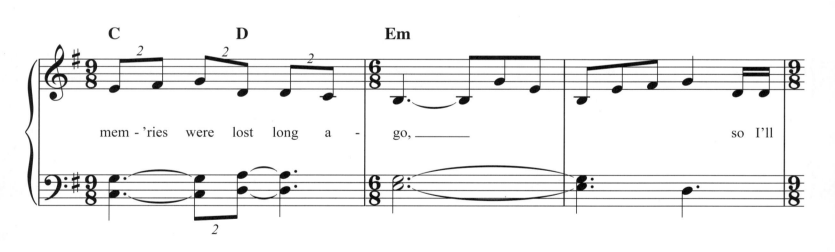

mem-'ries were lost long a - go, ____ so I'll

dance with these beau-ti-ful ghosts. ____

# MUNGOJERRIE AND RUMPLETEAZER

Music by ANDREW LLOYD WEBBER
Text by T.S. ELIOT

Mun - go - jer - rie and Rum - ple - tea - zer, we're a no - to - ri - ous cou - ple of cats. As

knock - a - bout clowns and quick change co - me - di - ans, tight - rope walk - ers and ac - ro - bats. We

Music Copyright © 1980 The Really Useful Group Ltd.
Text Copyright © 1939 T.S. Eliot; this edition of the text © 1980 Set Copyrights Ltd.
All Rights in the text Controlled by Faber and Faber Ltd.
International Copyright Secured   All Rights Reserved

have an ex-ten-sive re-pu-ta-tion, we made our home in Vic-to-ri-a Grove. This is

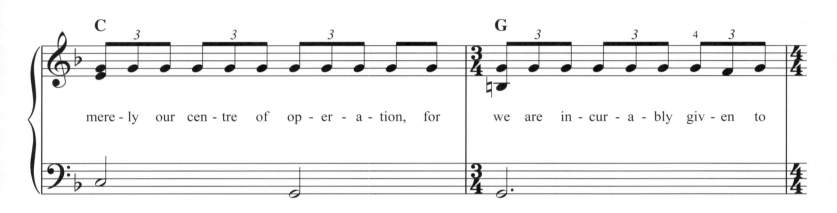

mere-ly our cen-tre of op-er-a-tion, for we are in-cur-a-bly giv-en to

rove. We are ver-y well known in Corn-wall Gar-dens, in

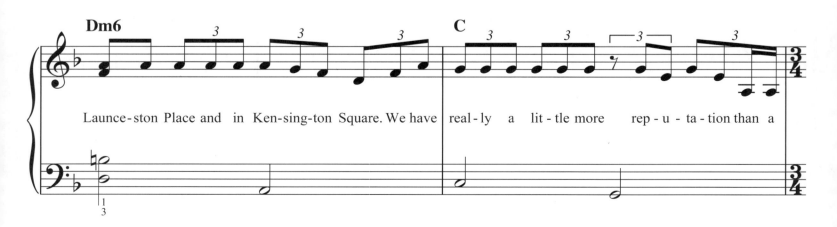

Launce-ston Place and in Ken-sing-ton Square. We have real-ly a lit-tle more rep-u-ta-tion than a

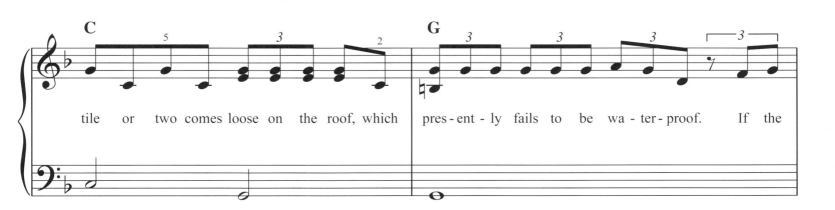

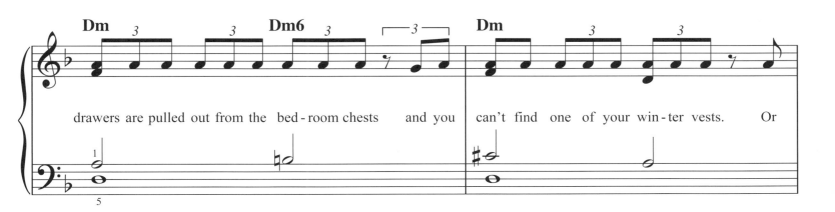

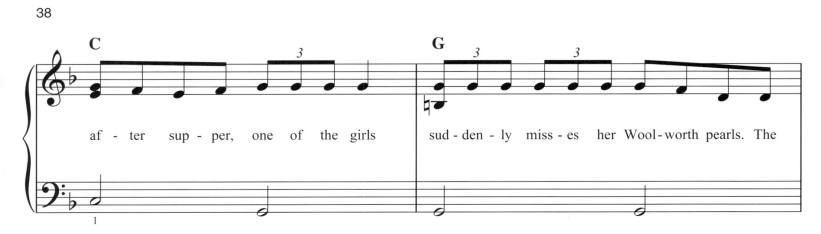

af - ter sup - per, one of the girls sud - den - ly miss - es her Wool - worth pearls. The

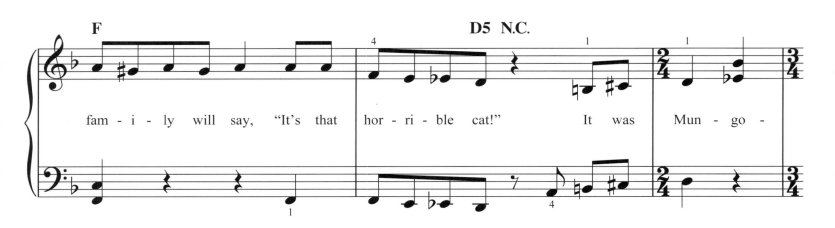

fam - i - ly will say, "It's that hor - ri - ble cat!" It was Mun - go -

jer - rie or Rum - ple - teaz - er. And

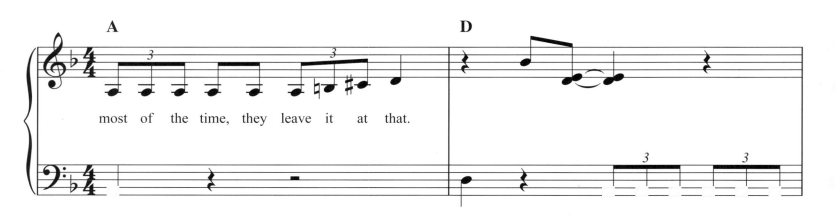

most of the time, they leave it at that.

Mun - go - jer - rie and Rum - ple - teaz - er have a ver - y un - us - u - al gift of the gab. We are

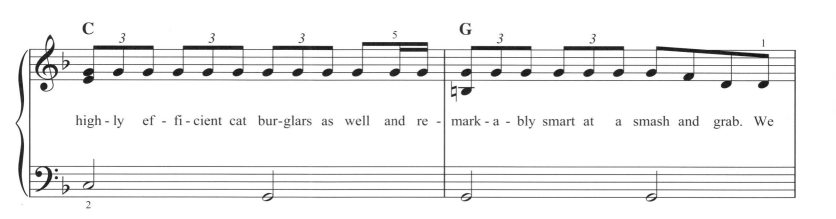

high - ly ef - fi - cient cat bur - glars as well and re - mark - a - bly smart at a smash and grab. We

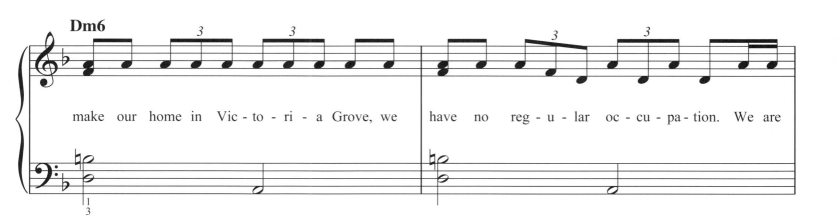

make our home in Vic - to - ri - a Grove, we have no reg - u - lar oc - cu - pa - tion. We are

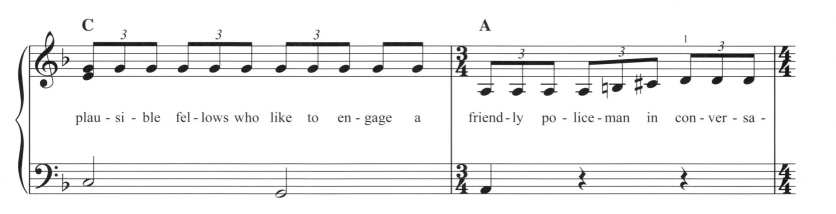

plau - si - ble fel - lows who like to en - gage a friend - ly po - lice - man in con - ver - sa -

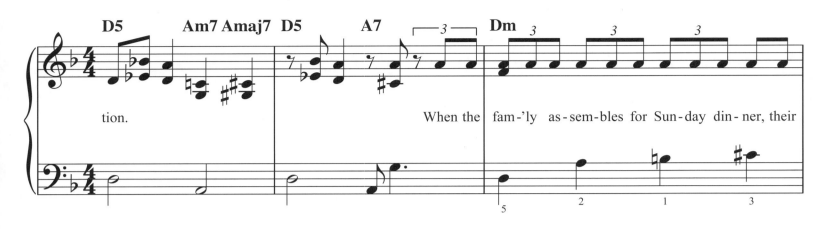

tion.          When the | fam-'ly as-sem-bles for Sun-day din-ner, their

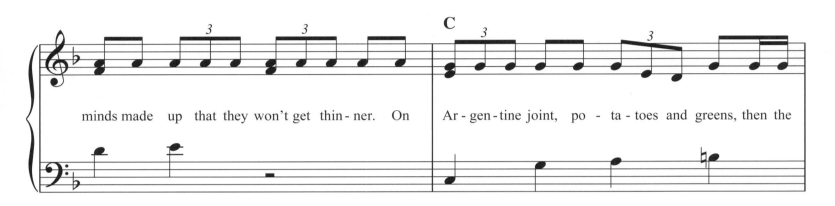

minds made  up  that they won't get thin-ner.  On | Ar-gen-tine joint,  po-ta-toes and greens, then the

cook will ap-pear from be-hind  the scenes and | say in   a voice that is bro-ken with sor-row, "I'm a-

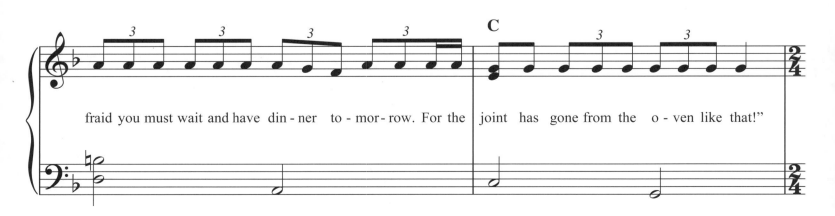

fraid you must wait and have din-ner  to-mor-row. For the | joint  has  gone from the  o-ven like that!"

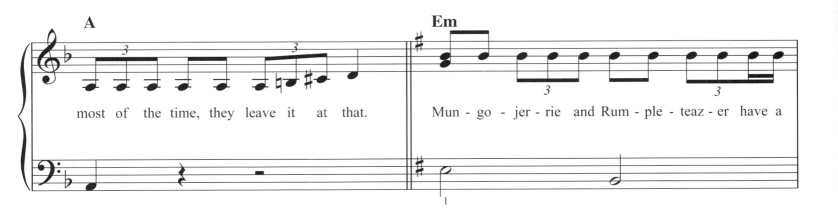

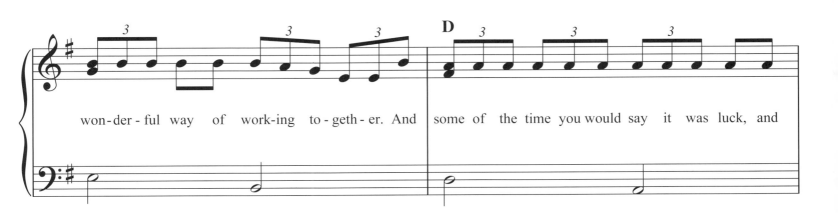

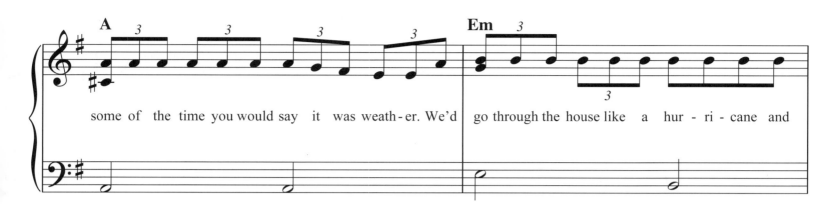

some of the time you would say it was weath-er. We'd | go through the house like a hur-ri-cane and

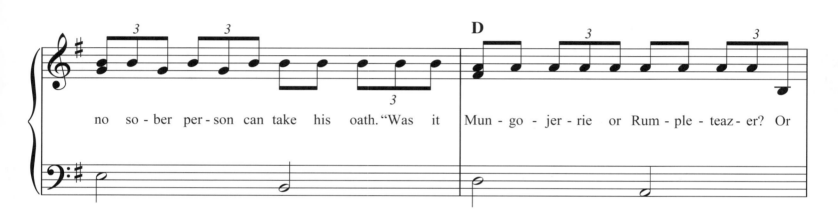

no so-ber per-son can take his oath. "Was it | Mun-go-jer-rie or Rum-ple-teaz-er? Or

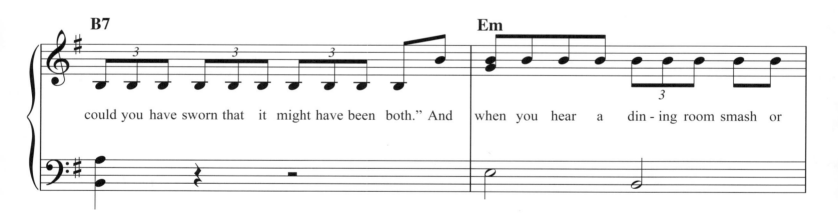

could you have sworn that it might have been both." And | when you hear a din-ing room smash or

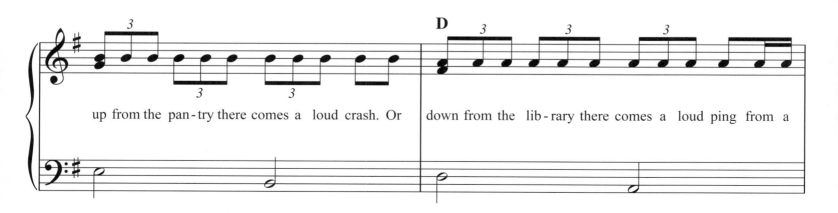

up from the pan-try there comes a loud crash. Or | down from the lib-rary there comes a loud ping from a

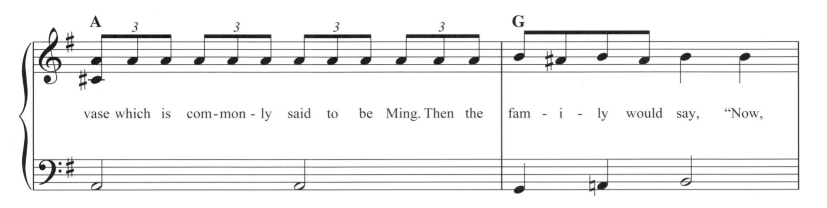

vase which is com-mon-ly said to be Ming. Then the fam - i - ly would say, "Now,

which was which cat?" It was Mun - go -

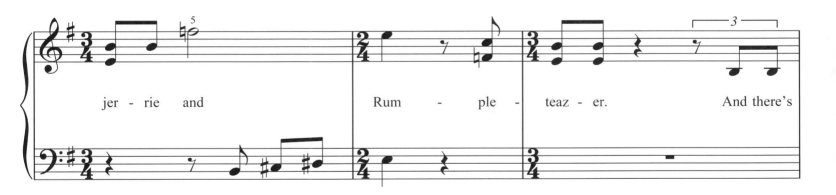

jer - rie and Rum - ple - teaz - er. And there's

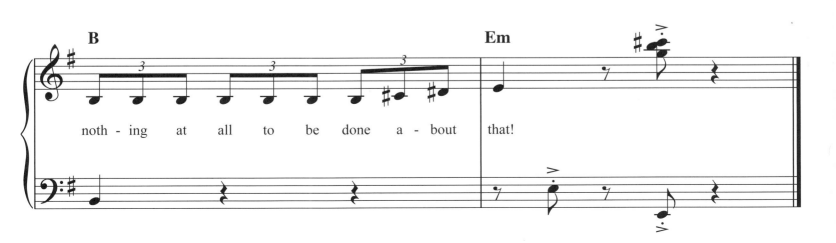

noth - ing at all to be done a - bout that!

# OLD DEUTERONOMY

Music by ANDREW LLOYD WEBBER
Text by T.S. ELIOT

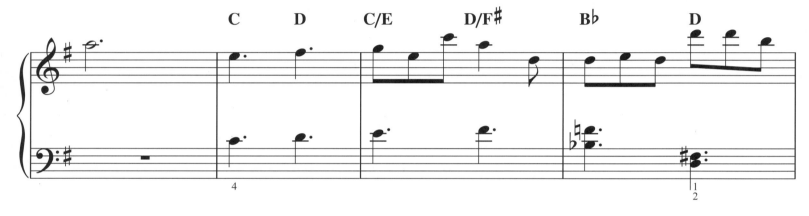

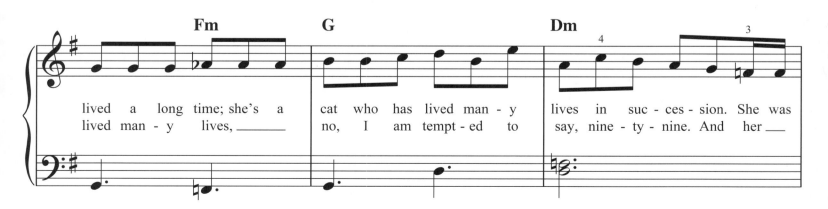

Music Copyright © 1980 Andrew Lloyd Webber licensed to the Really Useful Group Ltd.
Text Copyright © 1939 T.S. Eliot; this edition of the text © 1980 Set Copyrights Ltd.
All Rights in the text Controlled by Faber and Faber Ltd.
International Copyright Secured   All Rights Reserved

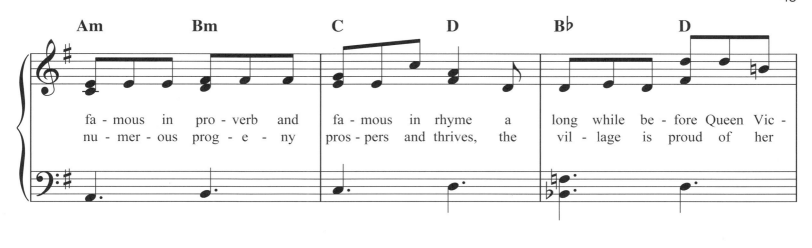

**Am**  **Bm**  **C**  **D**  **Bb**  **D**

fa - mous in pro - verb and  fa - mous in rhyme a  long while be - fore Queen Vic -
nu - mer - ous prog - e - ny  pros - pers and thrives, the  vil - lage is proud of her

**1.** **G**  **2.** **G**

to - ria's ac - ces - sion.  in her de - cline. At the  sight of that plac - id and

**F#/G**  **F/G**  **F#/G**  **G**

bland phys - i - og - no - my, when she  sits in the sun on the

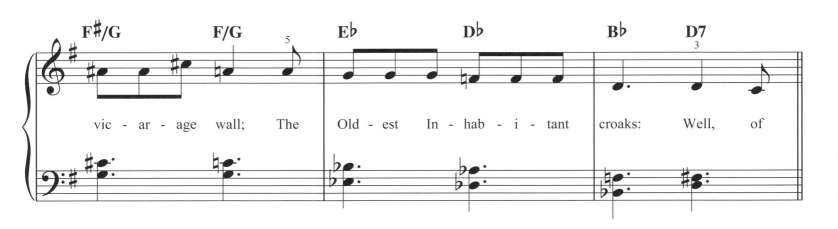

**F#/G**  **F/G**  **Eb**  **Db**  **Bb**  **D7**

vic - ar - age wall; The  Old - est In - hab - i - tant  croaks: Well, of

all things, can it be real - ly? Yes! No! Ho! Hi! Oh my

eye! My mind may be wan - der - ing but I con - fess, I be -

lieve it is Old Deu - ter - on - o - my. Well, of on - o - my. Well, of

all things, can it be real - ly? Yes! No! Ho! Hi! Oh my eye! My

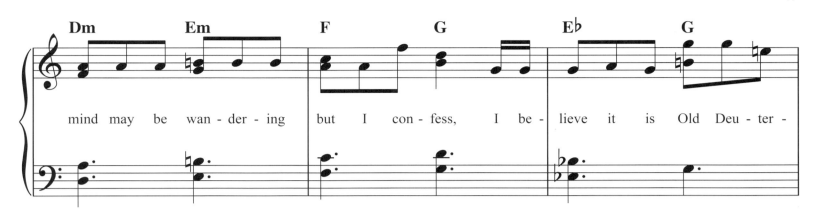

mind may be wan - der - ing but I con - fess, I be - lieve it is Old Deu - ter -

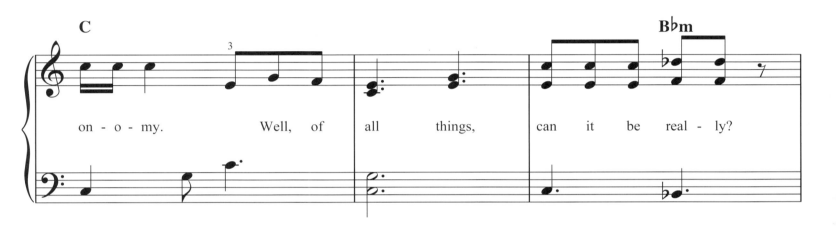

on - o - my. Well, of all things, can it be real - ly?

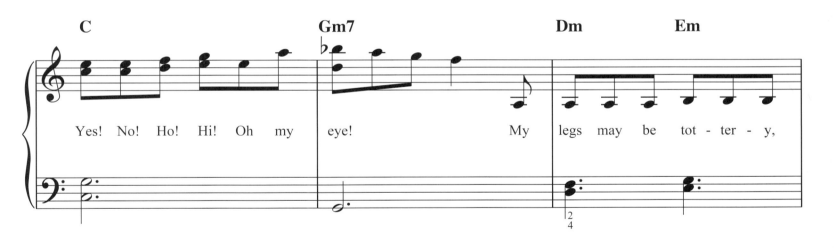

Yes! No! Ho! Hi! Oh my eye! My legs may be tot - ter - y,

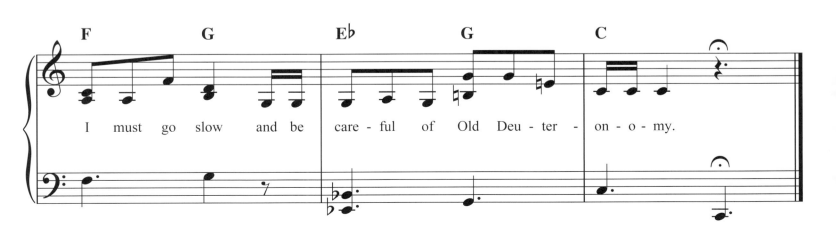

I must go slow and be care - ful of Old Deu - ter - on - o - my.

# GUS: THE THEATRE CAT

Music by ANDREW LLOYD WEBBER
Text by T.S. ELIOT

Music Copyright © 1981 Andrew Lloyd Webber licensed to The Really Useful Group Ltd.
Text Copyright © 1939 T.S. Eliot; this edition of the text © 1981 Set Copyrights Ltd.
All Rights in the text Controlled by Faber and Faber Ltd.
International Copyright Secured   All Rights Reserved

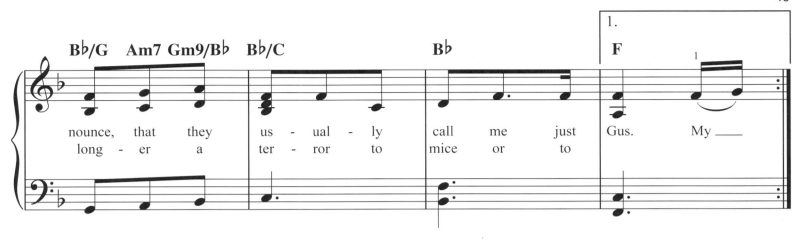

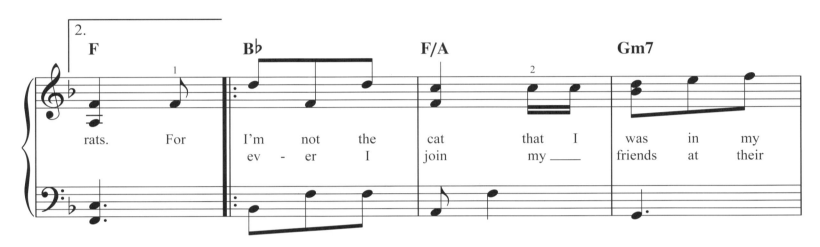

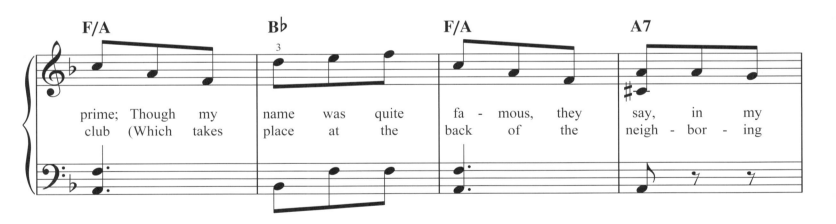

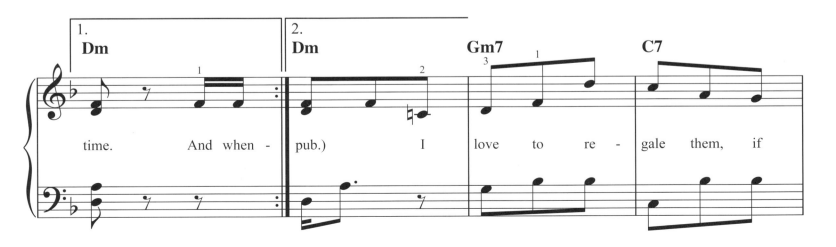

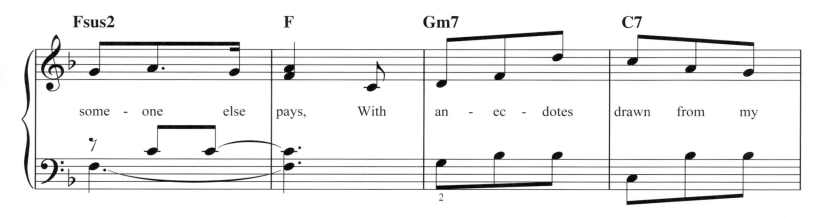

some-one else pays, With an-ec-dotes drawn from my

palm-i-est days. For I once was a Star of the
like to re-late my suc-

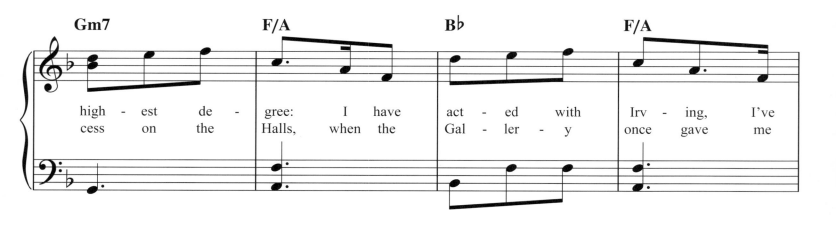

high-est de-gree: I have act-ed with Irv-ing, I've
cess on the Halls, when the Gal-ler-y once gave me

act-ed with Tree. And I grand-est cre-a-tion, as
sev-en cat-calls. But my

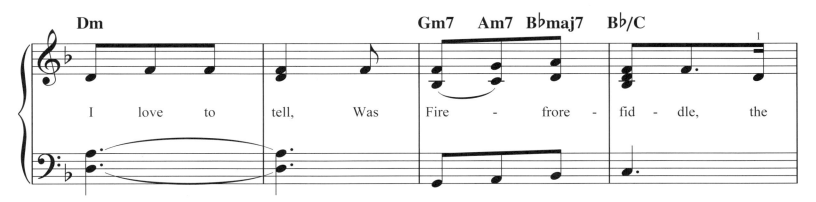

I love to tell, Was Fire - frore - fid - dle, the

Fiend of the Fell.

Then, if

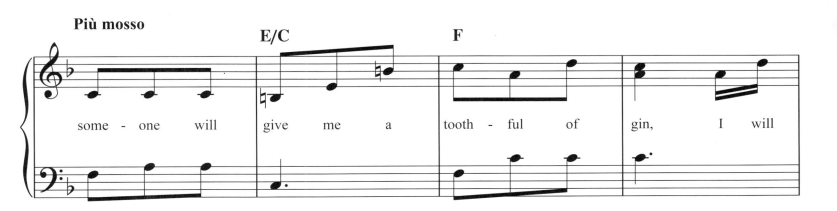

some - one will give me a tooth - ful of gin, I will

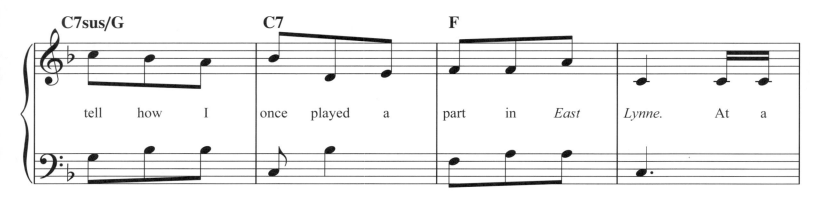

tell how I once played a part in *East Lynne.* At a

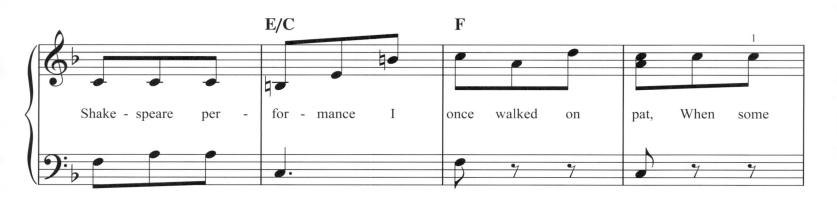

Shake - speare per - for - mance I once walked on pat, When some

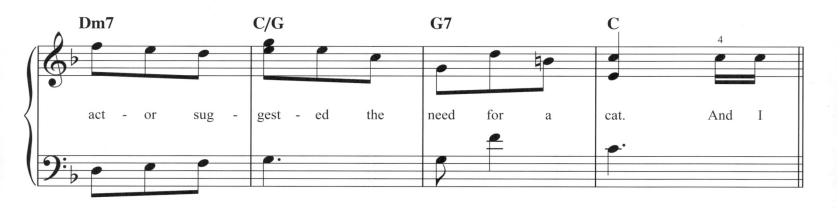

act - or sug - gest - ed the need for a cat. And I

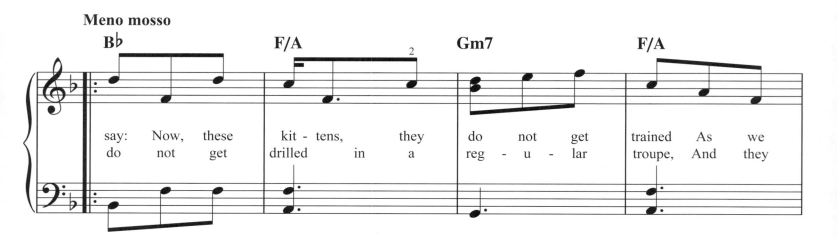

say: Now, these kit - tens, they do not get trained As we
do not get drilled in a reg - u - lar troupe, And they

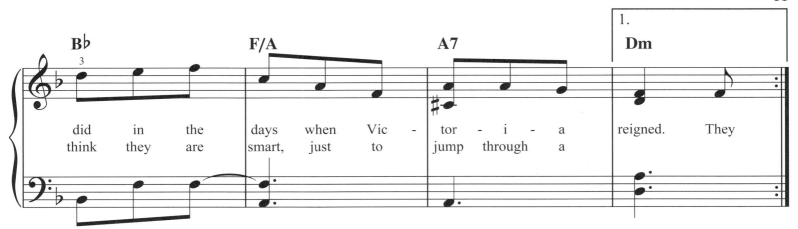

did in the / think they are the / days when Vic- / smart, just to / tor - i - a / jump through a / reigned. They / hoop.

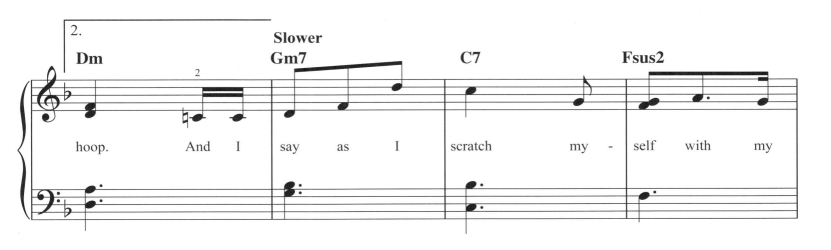

And I say as I scratch my - self with my

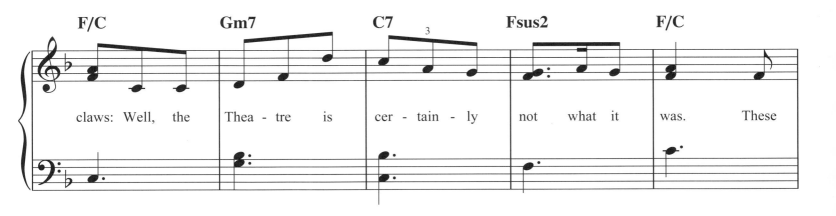

claws: Well, the Thea - tre is cer - tain - ly not what it was. These

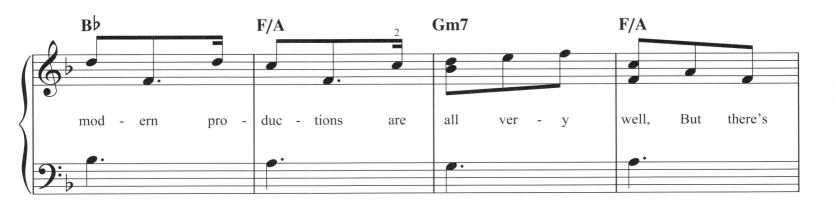

mod - ern pro - duc - tions are all ver - y well, But there's

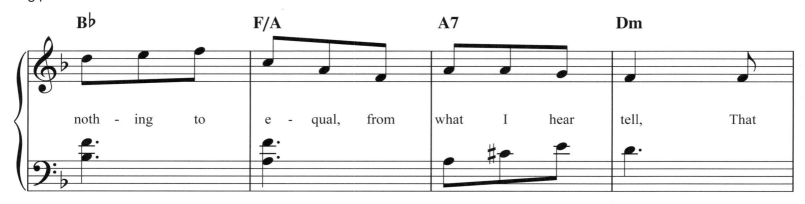

nothing to e - qual, from what I hear tell, That

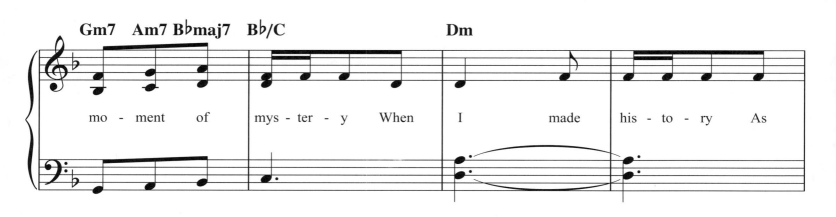

mo - ment of mys - ter - y When I made his - to - ry As

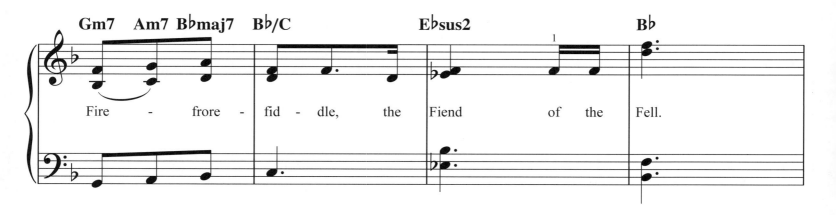

Fire - frore - fid - dle, the Fiend of the Fell.

# MACAVITY: THE MYSTERY CAT

Music by ANDREW LLOYD WEBBER
Text by T.S. ELIOT

Music Copyright © 1981 Andrew Lloyd Webber licensed to The Really Useful Group Ltd.
Text Copyright © 1939 T.S. Eliot; this edition of the text © 1981 Set Copyrights Ltd.
All Rights in the text Controlled by Faber and Faber Ltd.
International Copyright Secured   All Rights Reserved

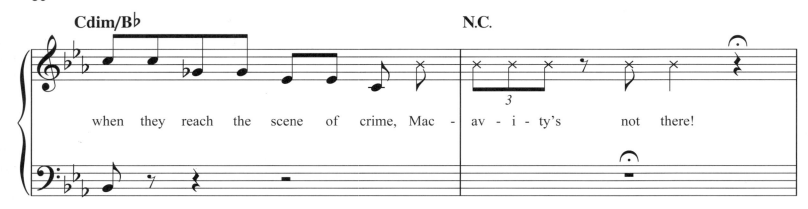

when they reach the scene of crime, Mac - av - i - ty's not there!

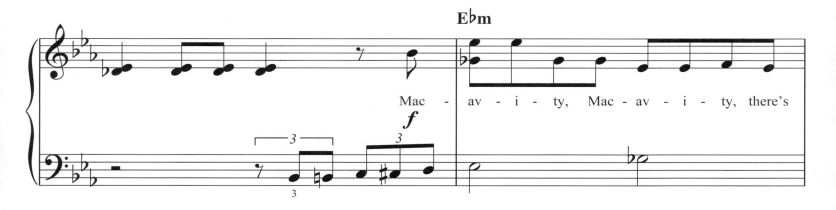

Mac - av - i - ty, Mac - av - i - ty, there's

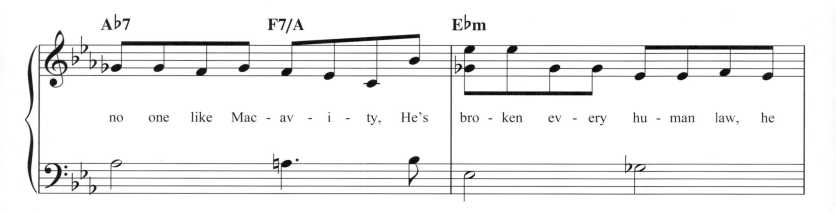

no one like Mac-av-i-ty, He's bro-ken ev-ery hu-man law, he

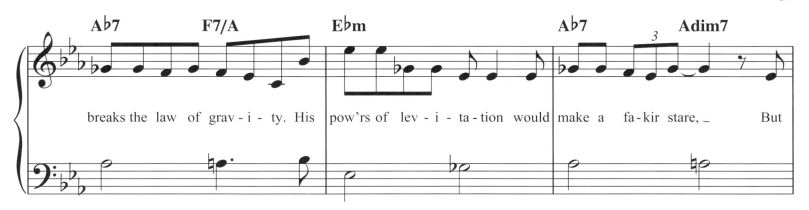

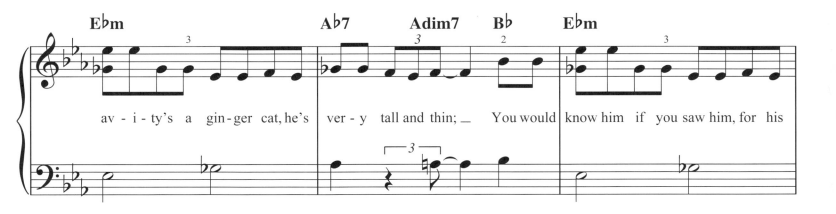

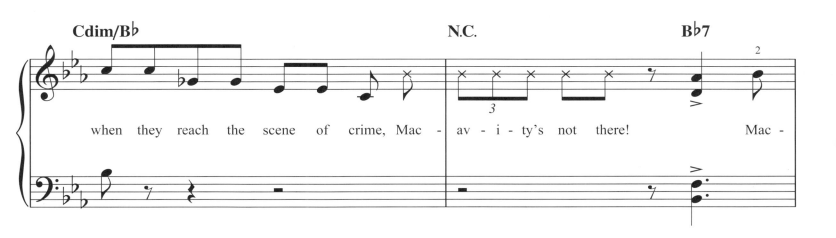

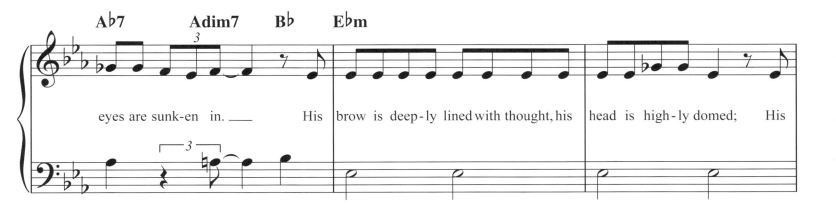

coat is dust - y from ne - glect, his whisk-ers are un-combed. He sways his head from side to side, with

move - ments like a snake; And when you think he's half a - sleep, he's

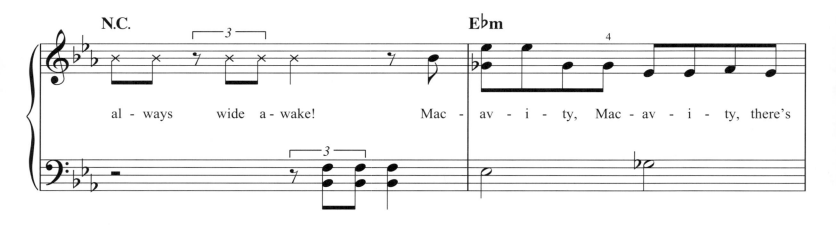

al - ways wide a - wake! Mac - av - i - ty, Mac - av - i - ty, there's

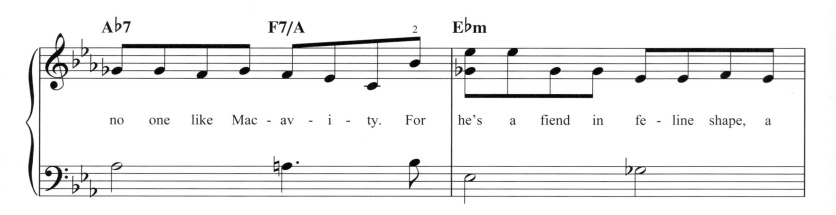

no one like Mac - av - i - ty. For he's a fiend in fe - line shape, a

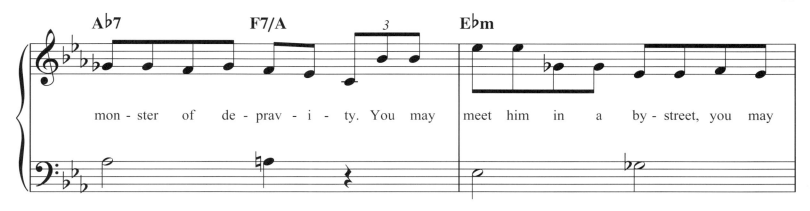

mon - ster of de - prav - i - ty. You may meet him in a by - street, you may

see him in the square; __ But when a crime's dis-cov-ered, then Mac - av - i - ty's not there! He's

out-ward-ly re-spec - ta - ble. __ (I know __ he cheats at cards.) And his

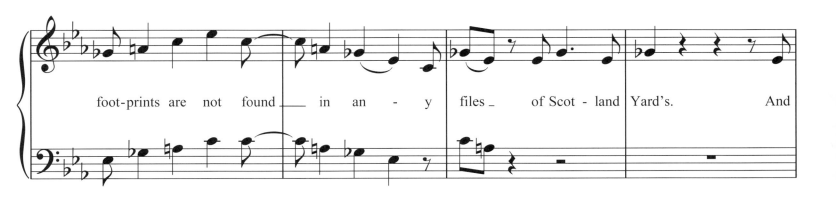

foot-prints are not found __ in an - y files __ of Scot - land Yard's. And

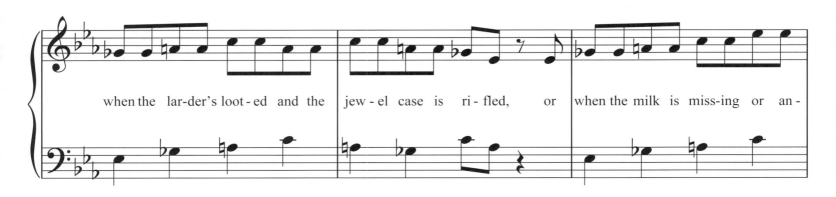

when the lar-der's loot-ed and the jew-el case is ri-fled, or when the milk is miss-ing or an-

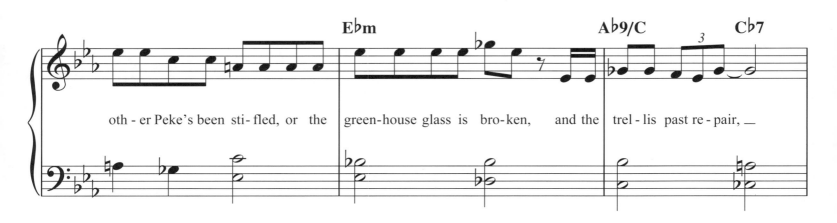

oth-er Peke's been sti-fled, or the green-house glass is bro-ken, and the trel-lis past re-pair, __

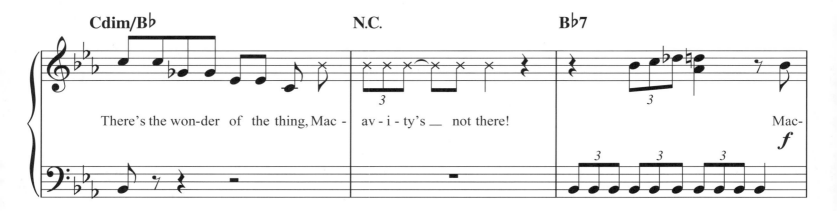

There's the won-der of the thing, Mac-av-i-ty's __ not there! Mac-

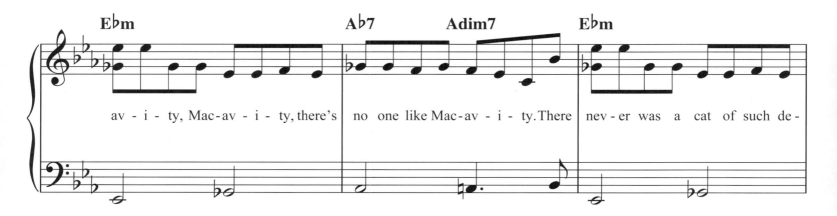

av-i-ty, Mac-av-i-ty, there's no one like Mac-av-i-ty. There nev-er was a cat of such de-

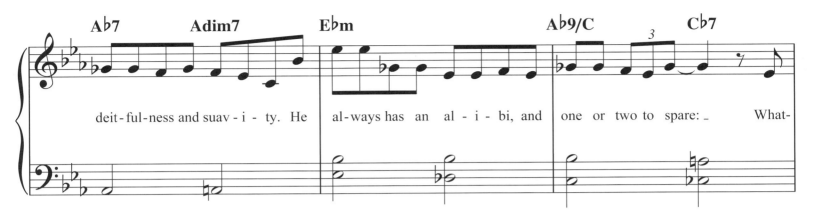

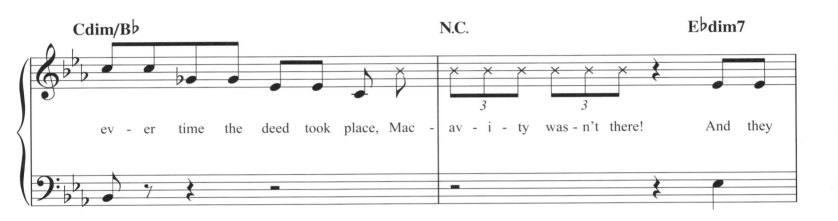

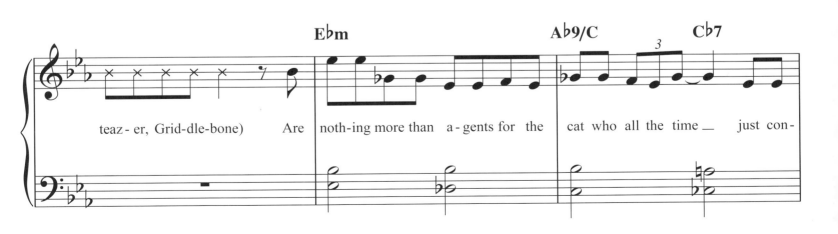

62

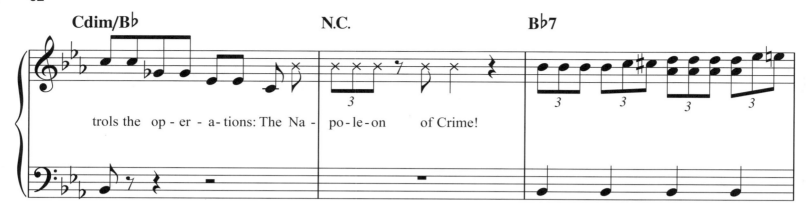

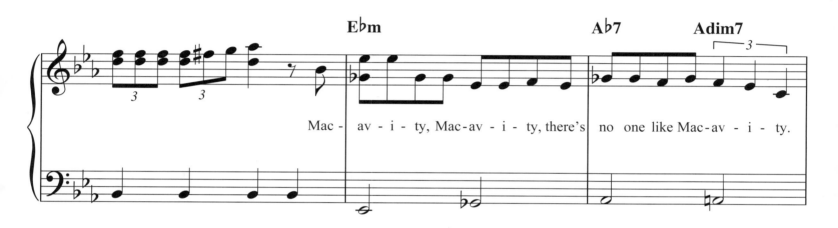

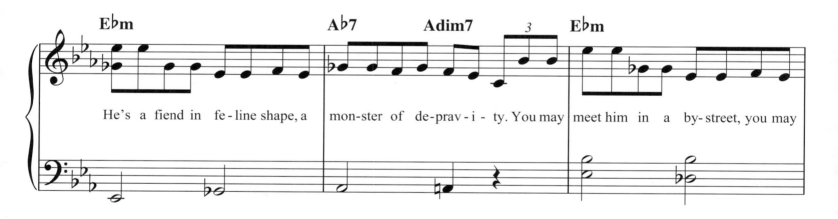

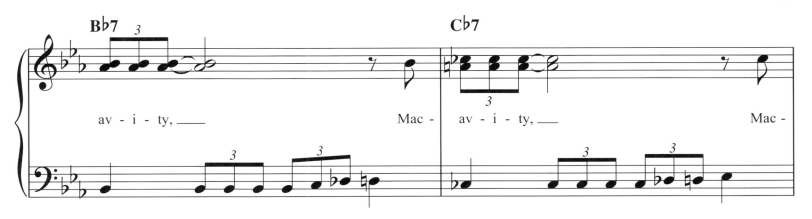

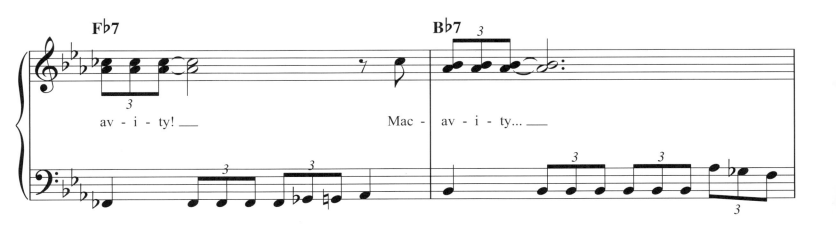

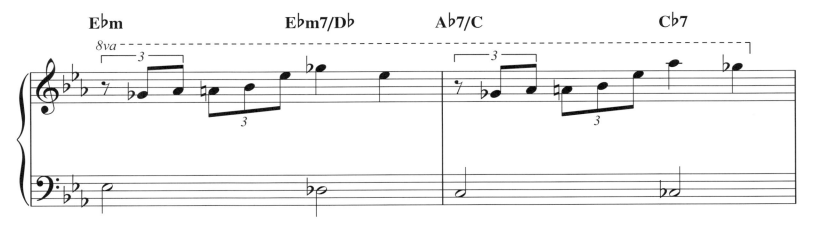

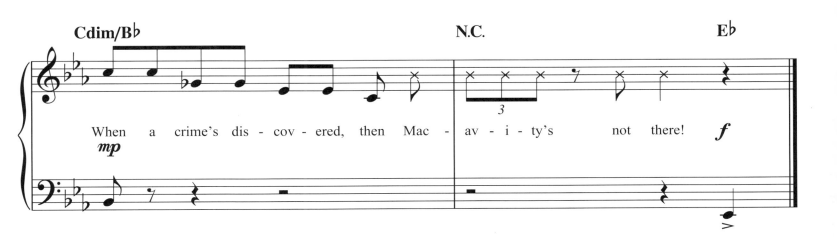

# SKIMBLESHANKS: THE RAILWAY CAT

Music by ANDREW LLOYD WEBBER
Text by T.S. ELIOT

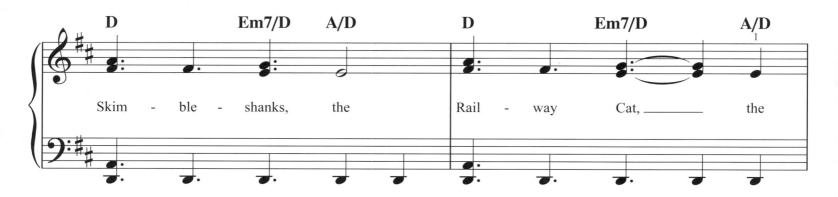

Skim - ble - shanks, the Rail - way Cat, _____ the

Cat of the Rail - way Train! There's a

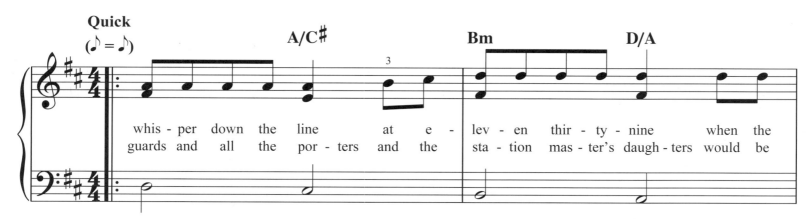

whis - per down the line at e - lev - en thir - ty - nine when the
guards and all the por - ters and the sta - tion mas - ter's daugh - ters would be

Music Copyright © 1980 Andrew Lloyd Webber licensed to The Really Useful Group Ltd.
Text Copyright © 1939 T.S. Eliot; this edition of the text © 1980 Set Copyrights Ltd.
All Rights in the text Controlled by Faber and Faber Ltd.
International Copyright Secured   All Rights Reserved

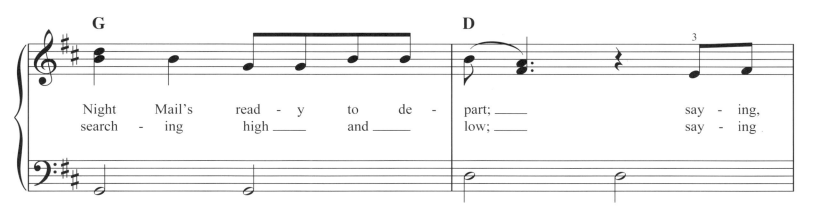

Night Mail's read - y to de - part; _____ say - ing,
search - ing high _____ and _____ low; _____ say - ing

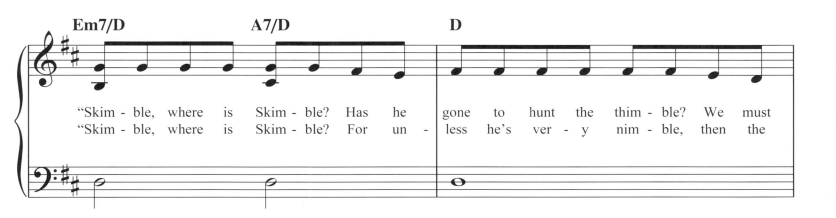

"Skim - ble, where is Skim - ble? Has he gone to hunt the thim - ble? We must
"Skim - ble, where is Skim - ble? For un - less he's ver - y nim - ble, then the

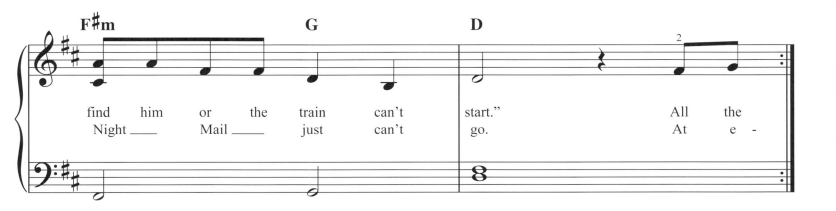

find him or the train can't start." All the
Night _____ Mail _____ just can't go. At e -

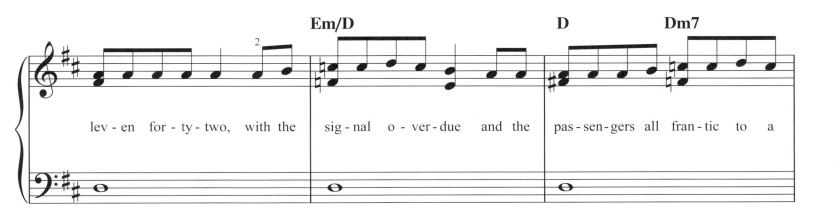

lev - en for - ty - two, with the sig - nal o - ver - due and the pas - sen - gers all fran - tic to a

man, that's when I would ap-pear and I'd saun-ter to the rear. I'd been

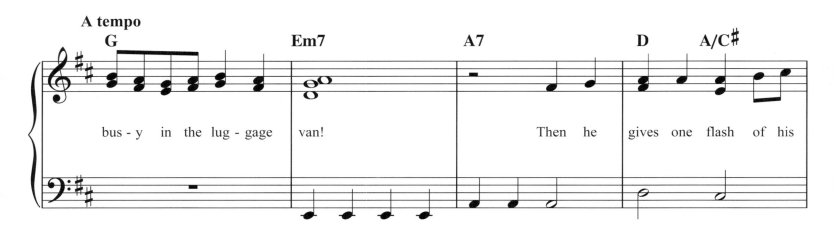

bus-y in the lug-gage van! Then he gives one flash of his

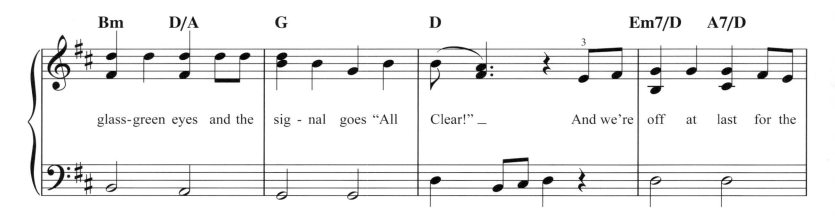

glass-green eyes and the sig-nal goes "All Clear!" And we're off at last for the

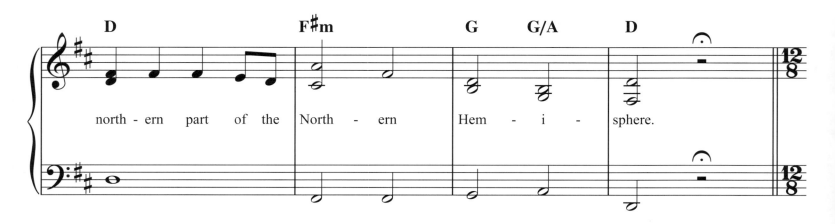

north-ern part of the North-ern Hem-i-sphere.

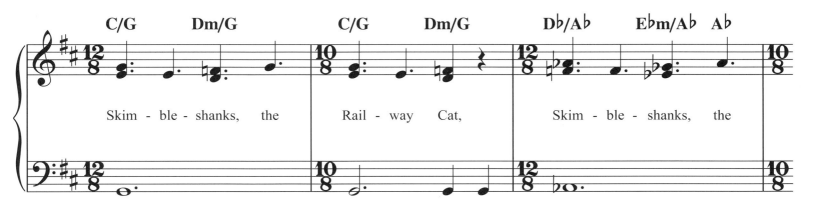

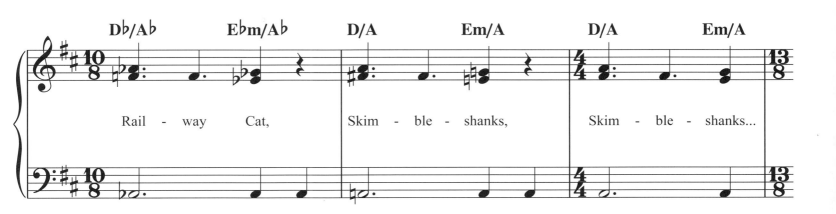

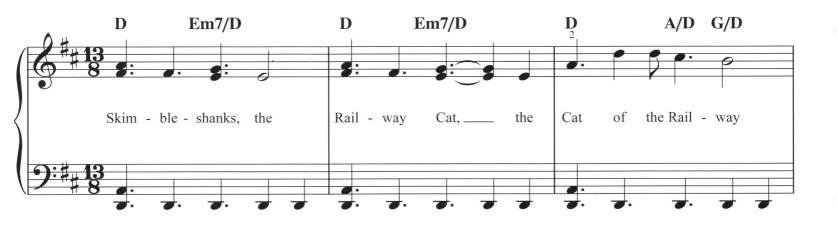

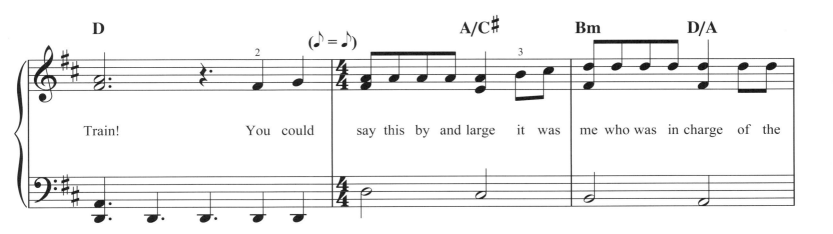

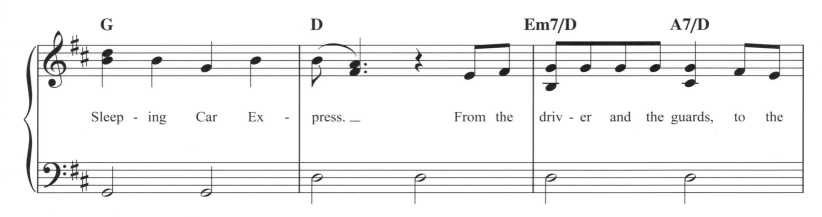

Sleep - ing Car Ex - press. ___ From the driv - er and the guards, to the

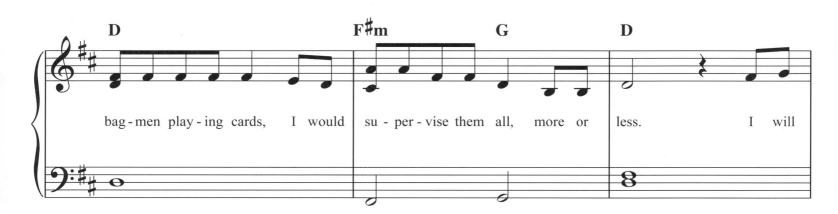

bag - men play - ing cards, I would su - per - vise them all, more or less. I will

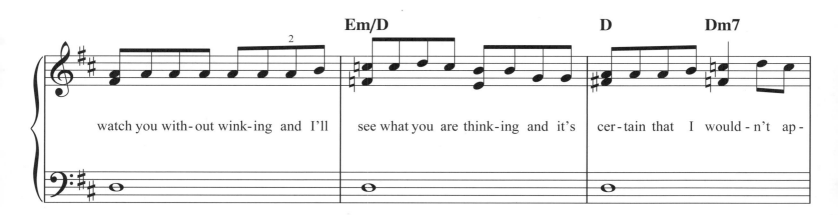

watch you with - out wink - ing and I'll see what you are think - ing and it's cer - tain that I would - n't ap -

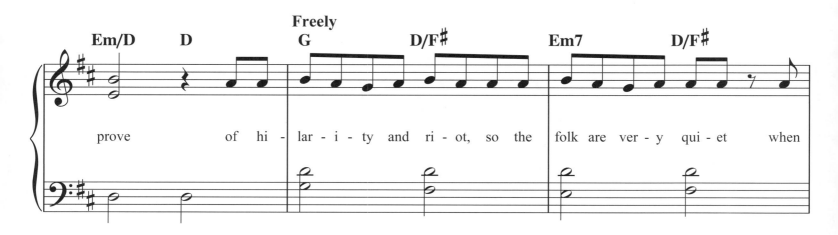

prove of hi - lar - i - ty and ri - ot, so the folk are ver - y qui - et when

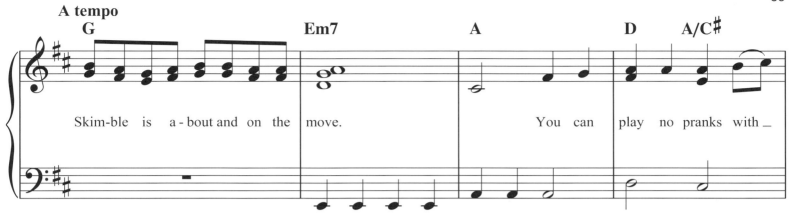

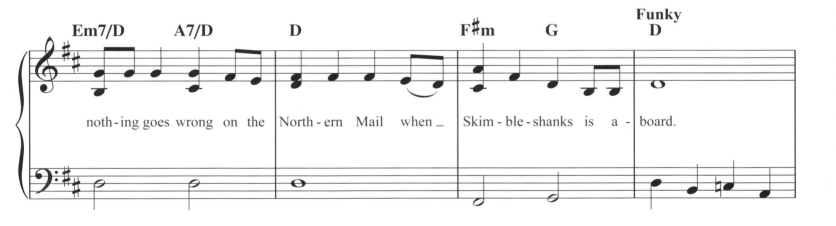

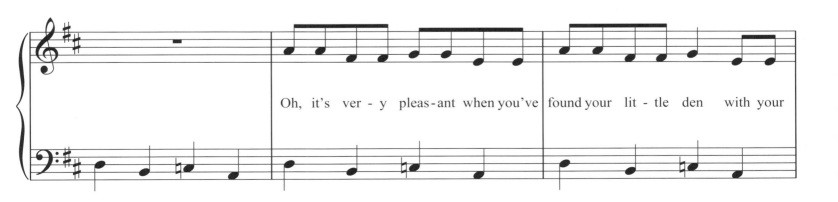

name writ-ten up on the door. And the berth is ver-y neat with a

new-ly fold-ed sheet and there's not a speck of dust on the floor. Then the

guard looked in po-lite-ly and would ask you ver-y bright-ly, "Do you like your morn-ing tea weak or

strong?" But I was just be-hind him and was read-y to re-mind him for

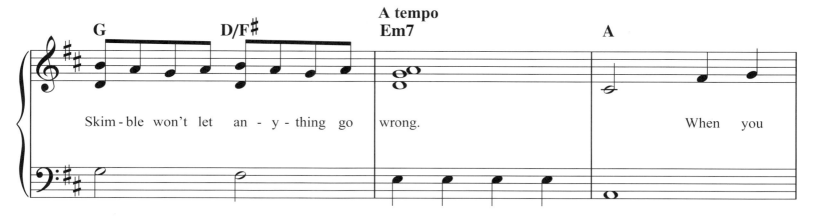

Skim-ble won't let an-y-thing go wrong. When you

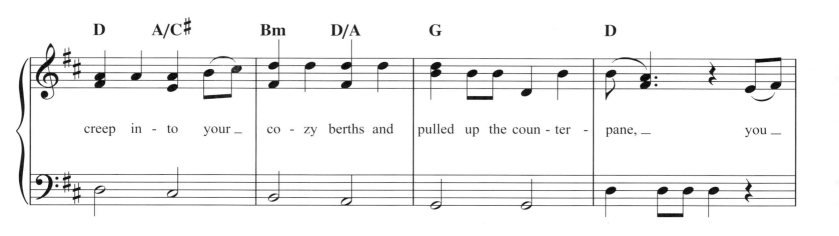

creep in-to your _ co-zy berths and pulled up the coun-ter - pane, _ you _

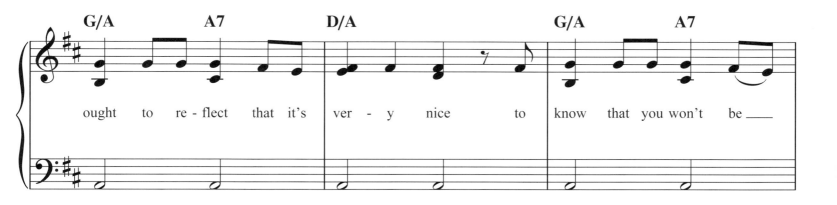

ought to re-flect that it's ver-y nice to know that you won't be ___

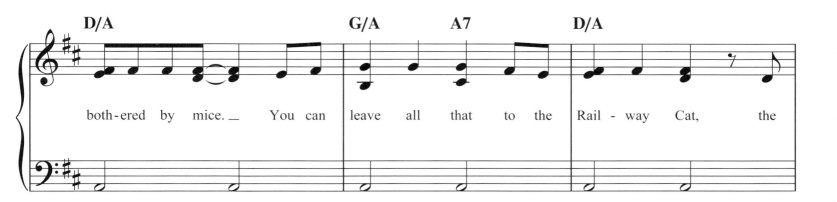

both-ered by mice. _ You can leave all that to the Rail - way Cat, the

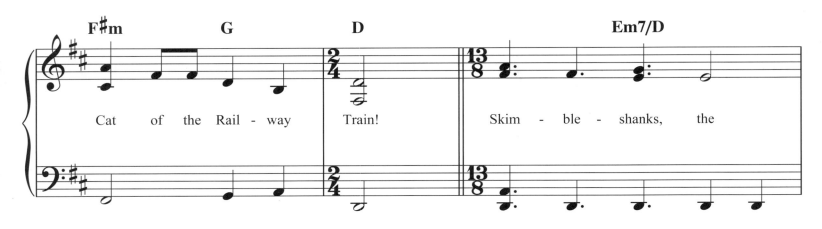

Cat of the Rail - way Train! Skim - ble - shanks, the

Rail - way Cat, ___ the Cat of the Rail - way Train! And he

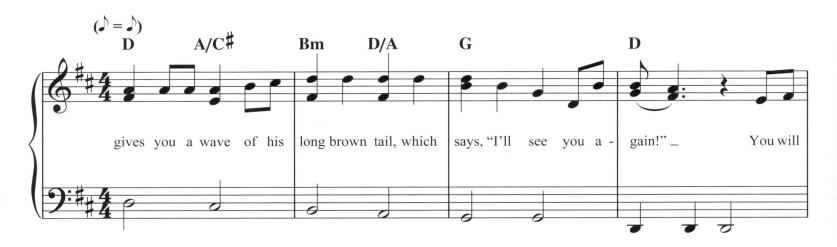

gives you a wave of his long brown tail, which says, "I'll see you a - gain!" ___ You will

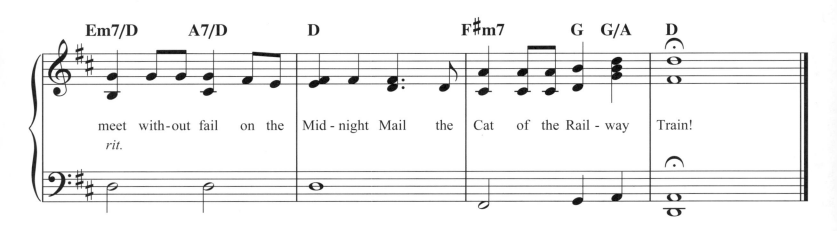

meet with-out fail on the Mid - night Mail the Cat of the Rail - way Train!

rit.

# MR. MISTOFFELEES

Music by ANDREW LLOYD WEBBER
Text by T.S. ELIOT

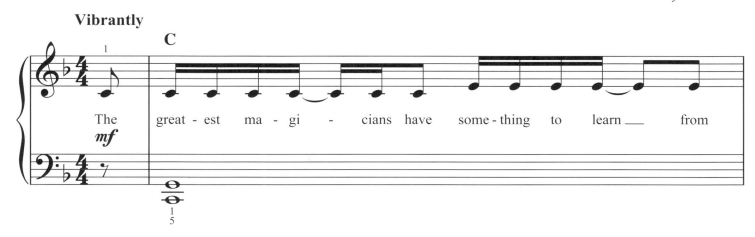

The great-est ma-gi- cians have some-thing to learn ___ from

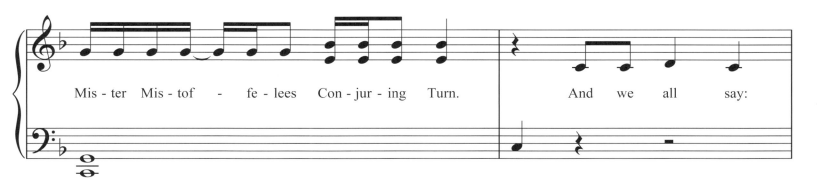

Mis-ter Mis-tof - fe-lees Con-jur-ing Turn. And we all say:

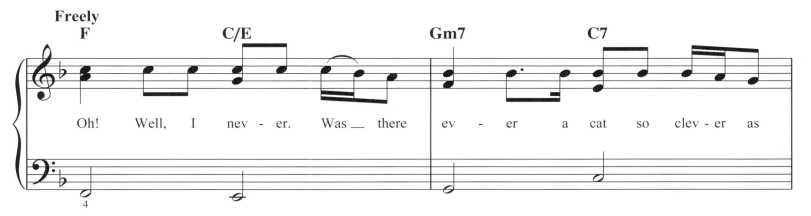

Oh! Well, I nev-er. Was ___ there ev-er a cat so clev-er as

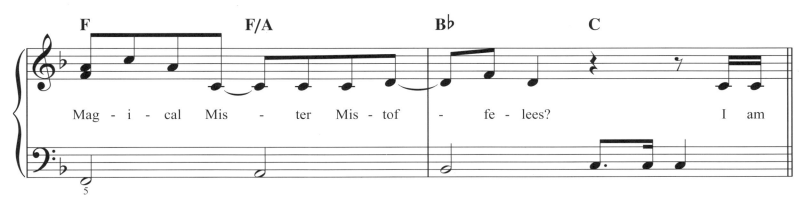

Mag-i-cal Mis - ter Mis-tof - fe-lees? I am

Music Copyright © 1980 Andrew Lloyd Webber licensed to The Really Useful Group Ltd.
Text Copyright © 1939 T.S. Eliot; this edition of the text © 1980 Set Copyrights Ltd.
All Rights in the text Controlled by Faber and Faber Ltd.
International Copyright Secured All Rights Reserved

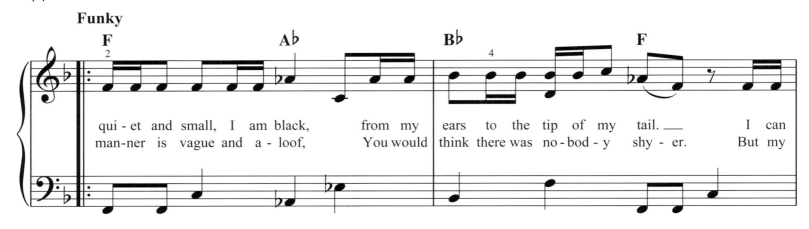

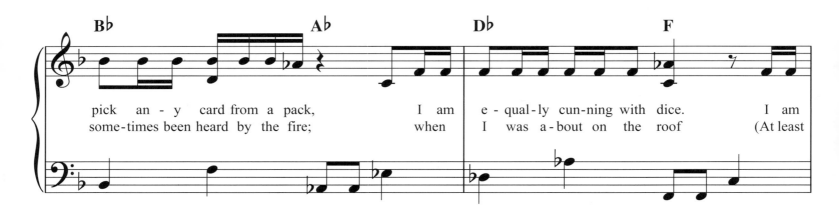

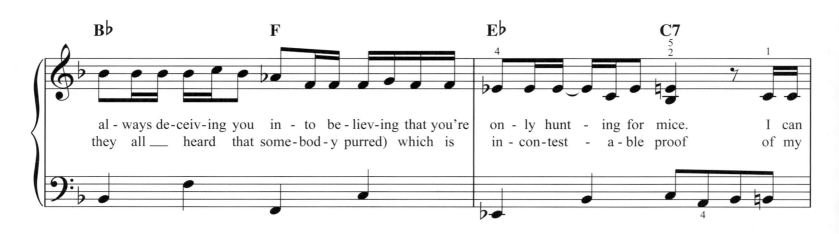

play an - y trick __ with a cork,     Or a | spoon and a bit of fish paste.     If you
sin - gu-lar mag - i - cal pow'rs.     And I've | known the __ fam-'ly to call     me __

look for a knife or a fork     And you | think it is mere - ly mis-placed;     You have
in from the gar - den for hours     when __ | I was a-sleep in the hall.     And

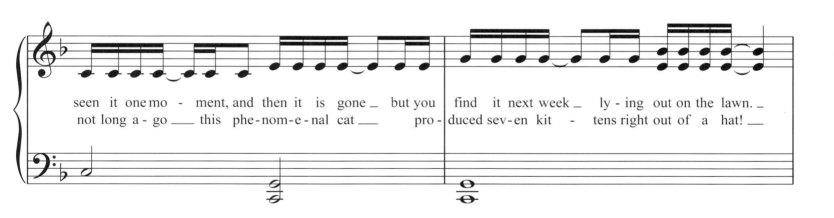

seen it one mo - ment, and then it is gone __ but you | find it next week __ ly - ing out on the lawn. __
not long a - go __ this phe-nom-e-nal cat __ | pro - duced sev-en kit - tens right out of a hat! __

**Vibrantly**
F     C/E     Gm7     C7

And we all say: }
And they all say: }
Oh! Well, I nev - er. Was __ there | ev - er a cat so clev-er as

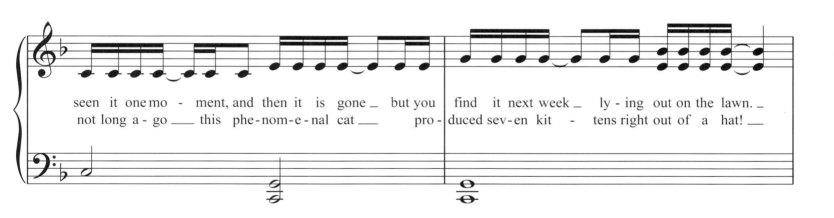

Mag - i - cal Mis - - ter Mis - tof - fe - lees?　　　　　　My

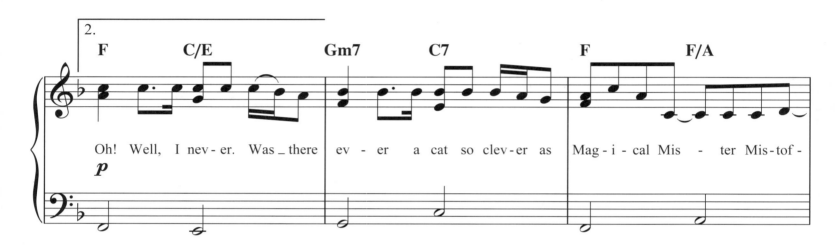

Oh! Well, I nev - er. Was ＿ there ev - er a cat so clev - er as Mag - i - cal Mis - - ter Mis - tof -

- fe - lees? We all say:　　Oh! Well, I nev - er. Was ＿ there ev - er a cat so clev - er as

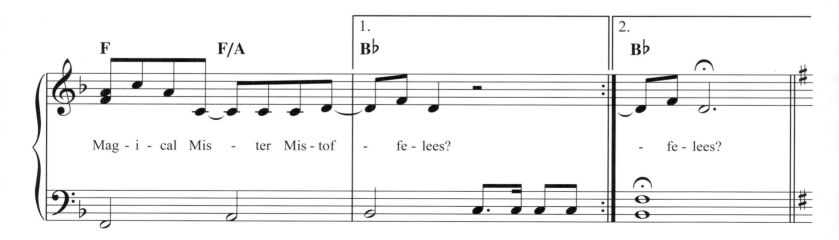

Mag - i - cal Mis - - ter Mis - tof - fe - lees?　　　　- fe - lees?

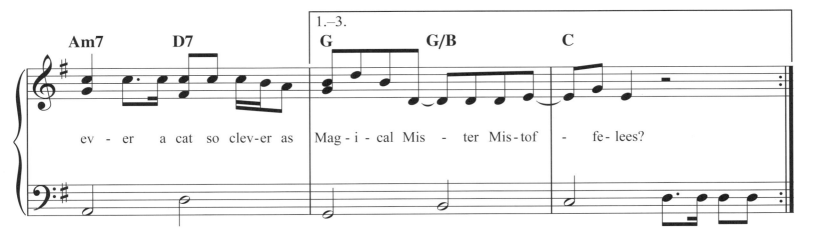

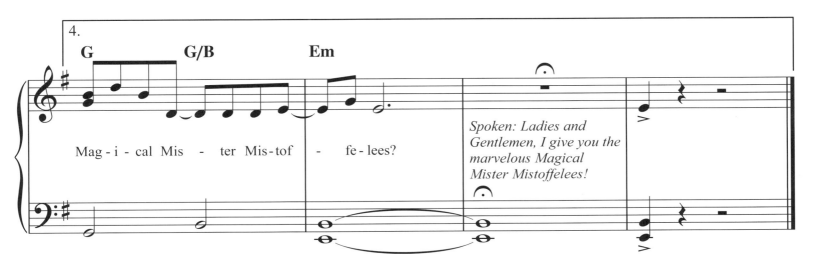

# MEMORY

Music by ANDREW LLOYD WEBBER
Text by TREVOR NUNN after T.S. ELIOT

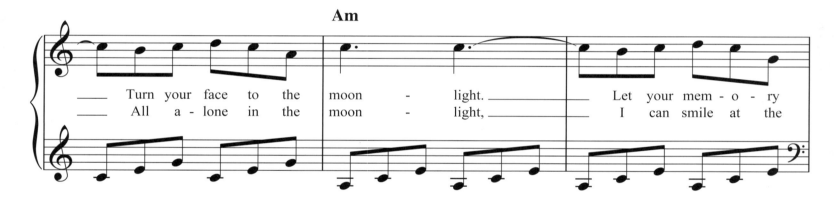

Music Copyright © 1981 Andrew Lloyd Webber licensed to The Really Useful Group Ltd.
Text Copyright © 1981 Trevor Nunn and Set Copyrights Ltd.
All Rights in the text Controlled by Faber and Faber Ltd.
International Copyright Secured   All Rights Reserved

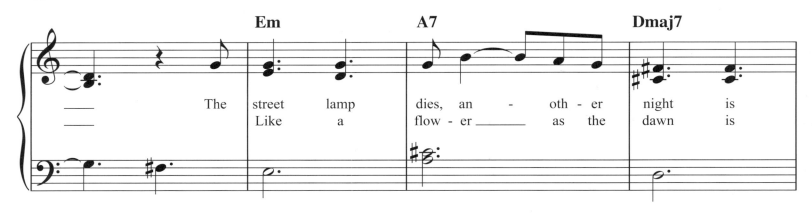

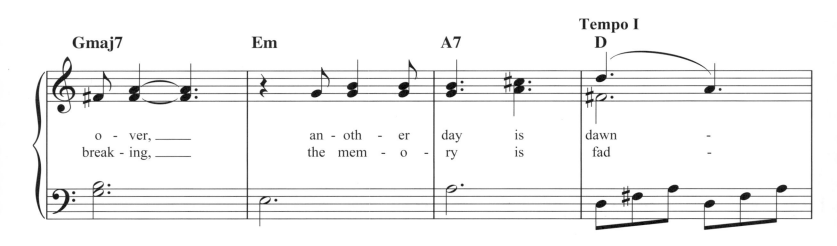

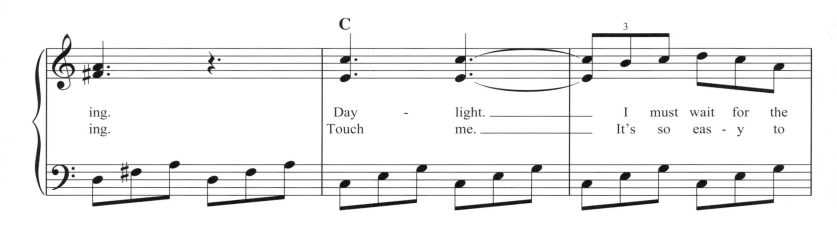

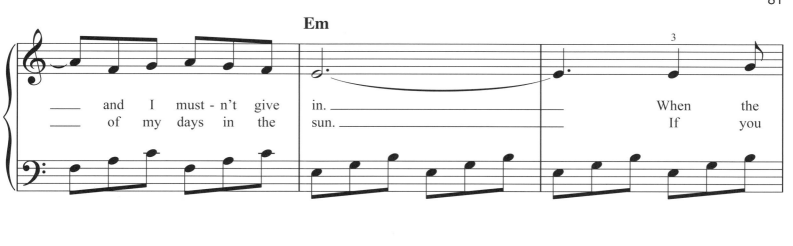

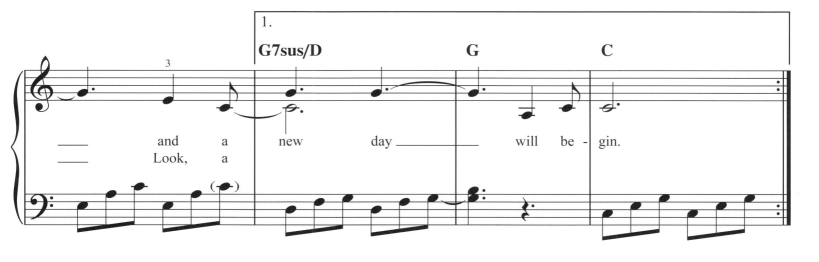

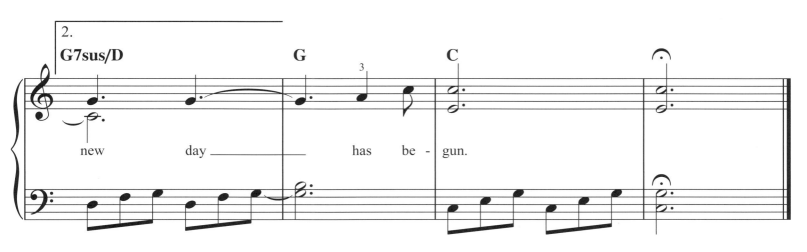

# THE AD-DRESSING OF CATS

Music by ANDREW LLOYD WEBBER
Text by T.S. ELIOT

**Moderate Admirable March**

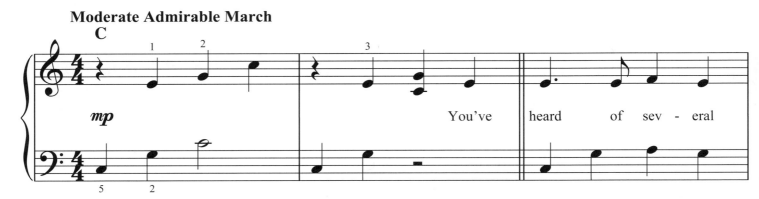

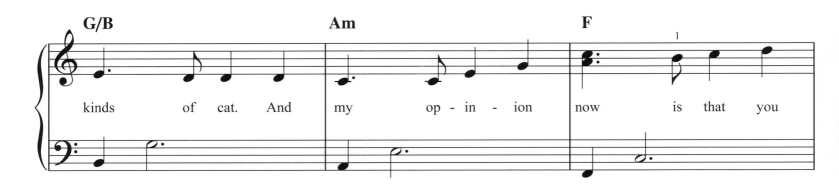

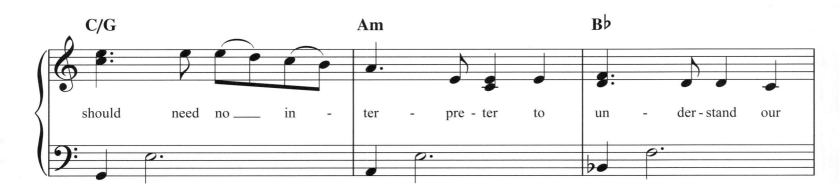

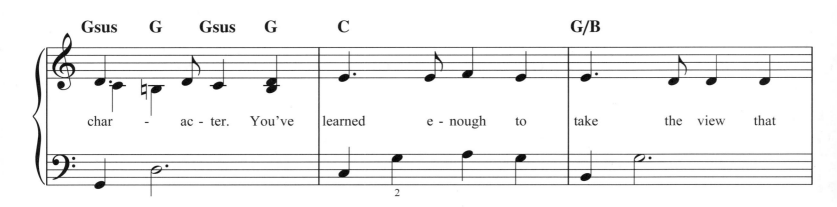

Music Copyright © 1981 Andrew Lloyd Webber licensed to The Really Useful Group Ltd.
Text Copyright © 1939 T.S. Eliot; this edition of the text © 1981 Set Copyrights Ltd.
All Rights in the text Controlled by Faber and Faber Ltd.
International Copyright Secured   All Rights Reserved

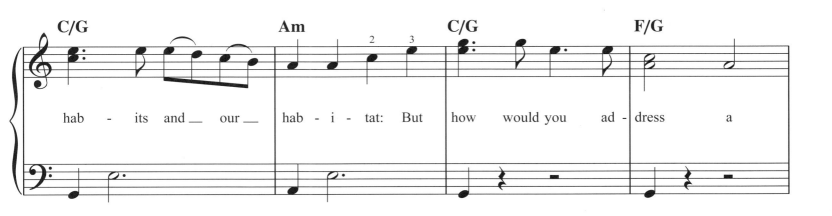

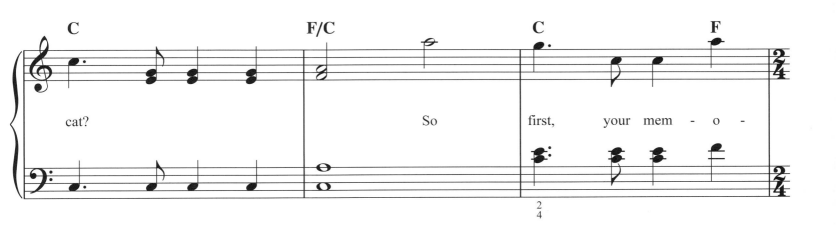

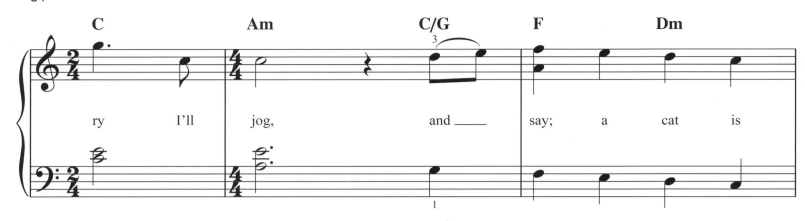

ry     I'll      jog,                    and ___ say;   a cat is

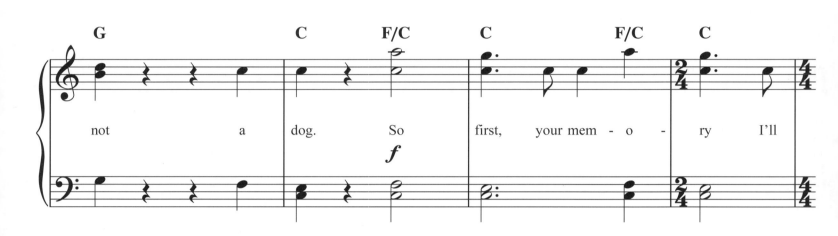

not               a       dog.   So       first,  your mem - o - ry  I'll

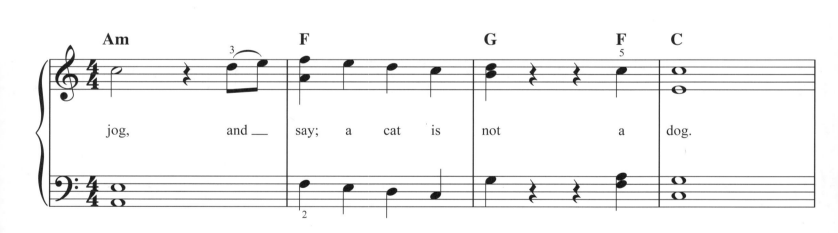

jog,               and __ say;  a cat  is   not             a       dog.

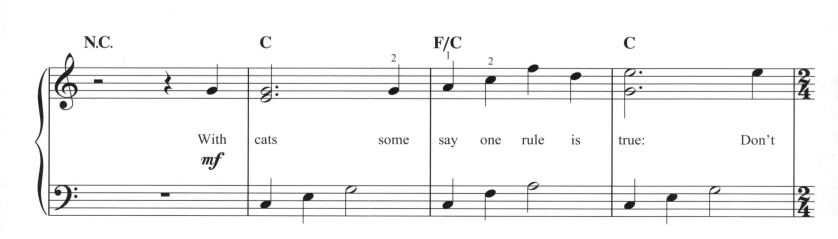

With   cats     some    say  one  rule  is     true:       Don't

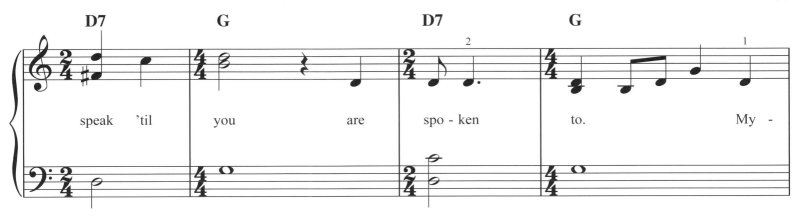

speak 'til you are spo - ken to. My -

self, I do not hold with that. I say, you should ad -

dress a cat. But al - ways bear in mind that he re -

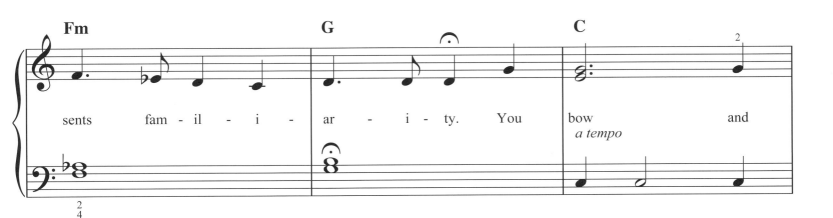

sents fam - il - i - ar - i - ty. You bow and

tak - ing off your hat, ad - dress him in this

form: O Cat. O Cat. Be - fore a cat will

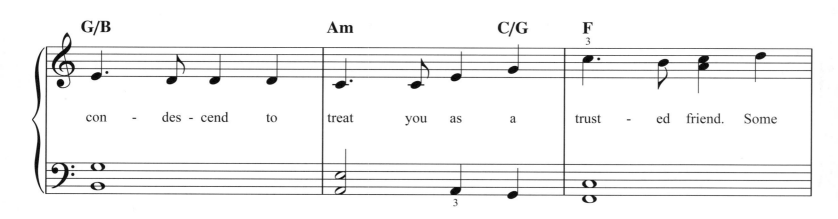

con - des - cend to treat you as a trust - ed friend. Some

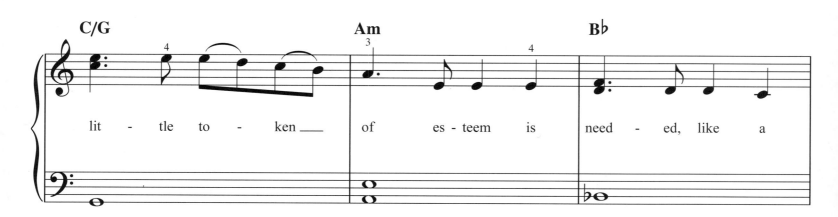

lit - tle to - ken of es - teem is need - ed, like a

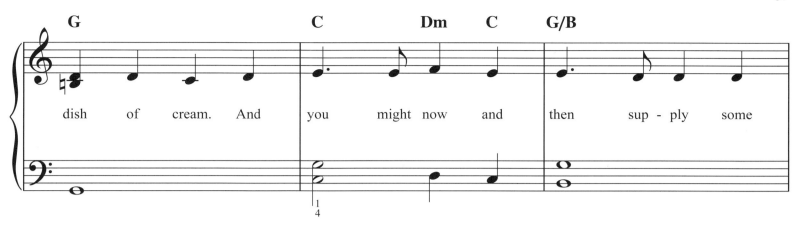

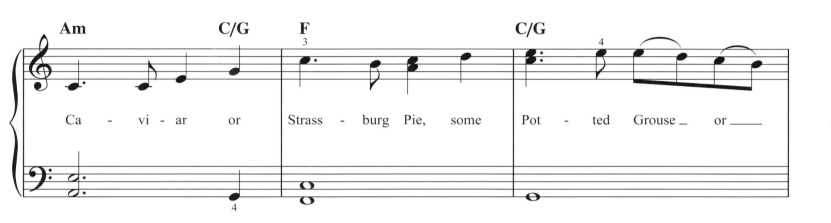

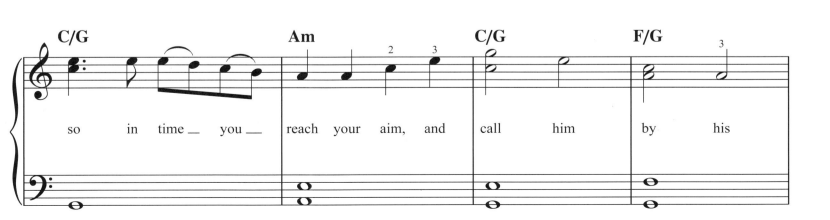

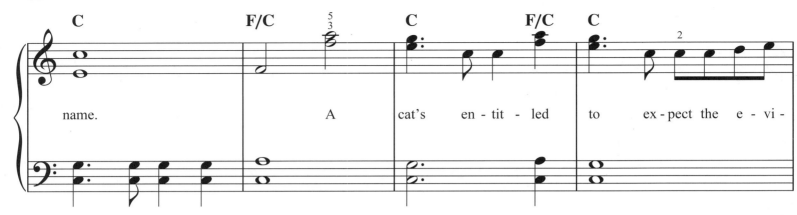

name.      A    cat's   en - tit - led    to    ex - pect the   e - vi -

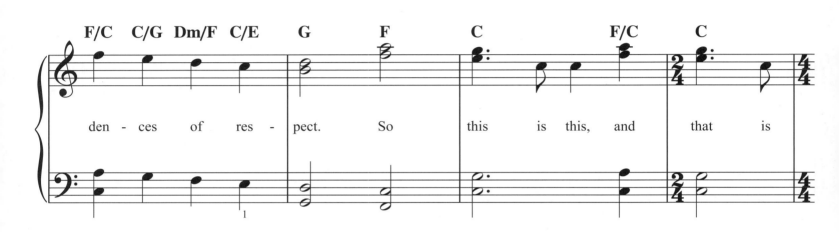

den - ces    of   res - pect.    So     this     is   this,   and     that    is

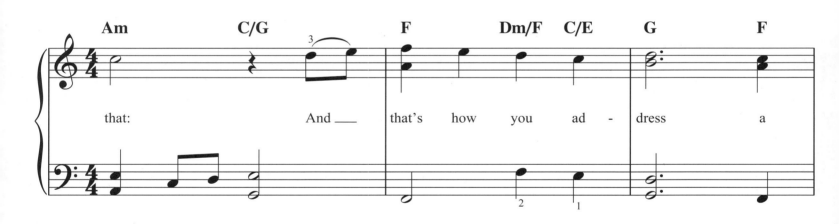

that:       And ___ that's   how   you   ad - dress     a

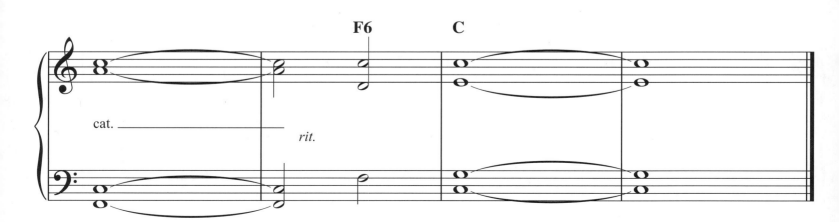

cat. _____     *rit.*